C-3374   CAREER EXAMINATION SERIES

This is your
PASSBOOK for...

Senior Office Typist

Test Preparation Study Guide
Questions & Answers

COPYRIGHT NOTICE

This book is SOLELY intended for, is sold ONLY to, and its use is RESTRICTED to individual, bona fide applicants or candidates who qualify by virtue of having seriously filed applications for appropriate license, certificate, professional and/or promotional advancement, higher school matriculation, scholarship, or other legitimate requirements of education and/or governmental authorities.

This book is NOT intended for use, class instruction, tutoring, training, duplication, copying, reprinting, excerption, or adaptation, etc., by:

1) Other publishers
2) Proprietors and/or Instructors of "Coaching" and/or Preparatory Courses
3) Personnel and/or Training Divisions of commercial, industrial, and governmental organizations
4) Schools, colleges, or universities and/or their departments and staffs, including teachers and other personnel
5) Testing Agencies or Bureaus
6) Study groups which seek by the purchase of a single volume to copy and/or duplicate and/or adapt this material for use by the group as a whole without having purchased individual volumes for each of the members of the group
7) Et al.

Such persons would be in violation of appropriate Federal and State statutes.

PROVISION OF LICENSING AGREEMENTS – Recognized educational, commercial, industrial, and governmental institutions and organizations, and others legitimately engaged in educational pursuits, including training, testing, and measurement activities, may address request for a licensing agreement to the copyright owners, who will determine whether, and under what conditions, including fees and charges, the materials in this book may be used them. In other words, a licensing facility exists for the legitimate use of the material in this book on other than an individual basis. However, it is asseverated and affirmed here that the material in this book CANNOT be used without the receipt of the express permission of such a licensing agreement from the Publishers. Inquiries re licensing should be addressed to the company, attention rights and permissions department.

All rights reserved, including the right of reproduction in whole or in part, in any form or by any means, electronic or mechanical, including photocopying, recording, or by any information storage and retrieval system, without permission in writing from the Publisher.

Copyright © 2025 by
National Learning Corporation

212 Michael Drive, Syosset, NY 11791
(516) 921-8888 • www.passbooks.com
E-mail: info@passbooks.com

PASSBOOK® SERIES

THE *PASSBOOK® SERIES* has been created to prepare applicants and candidates for the ultimate academic battlefield – the examination room.

At some time in our lives, each and every one of us may be required to take an examination – for validation, matriculation, admission, qualification, registration, certification, or licensure.

Based on the assumption that every applicant or candidate has met the basic formal educational standards, has taken the required number of courses, and read the necessary texts, the *PASSBOOK® SERIES* furnishes the one special preparation which may assure passing with confidence, instead of failing with insecurity. Examination questions – together with answers – are furnished as the basic vehicle for study so that the mysteries of the examination and its compounding difficulties may be eliminated or diminished by a sure method.

This book is meant to help you pass your examination provided that you qualify and are serious in your objective.

The entire field is reviewed through the huge store of content information which is succinctly presented through a provocative and challenging approach – the question-and-answer method.

A climate of success is established by furnishing the correct answers at the end of each test.

You soon learn to recognize types of questions, forms of questions, and patterns of questioning. You may even begin to anticipate expected outcomes.

You perceive that many questions are repeated or adapted so that you can gain acute insights, which may enable you to score many sure points.

You learn how to confront new questions, or types of questions, and to attack them confidently and work out the correct answers.

You note objectives and emphases, and recognize pitfalls and dangers, so that you may make positive educational adjustments.

Moreover, you are kept fully informed in relation to new concepts, methods, practices, and directions in the field.

You discover that you are actually taking the examination all the time: you are preparing for the examination by "taking" an examination, not by reading extraneous and/or supererogatory textbooks.

In short, this PASSBOOK®, used directedly, should be an important factor in helping you to pass your test.

SENIOR OFFICE TYPIST

DISTINGUISHING FEATURES OF WORK
Senior Office Typists work with a limited degree of independence on a variety of office clerical and keyboarding tasks, as supervisors of small clerical sub-units, at public counters as information clerks, and perform other related duties. Senior Office Typists are located in courts of every jurisdiction. County Clerks' and Commissioners of Jurors' Offices, law libraries, and administrative offices and auxiliary agencies in the Unified Court System.

WRITTEN TEST

SUBJECT OF EXAMINATION
This examination is a written multiple-choice test designed to test for knowledge, skills and abilities in such areas as:

1. <u>Understanding and Interpreting Written Material</u>
   These questions are designed to test the candidates' ability to comprehend written material. The candidates will be provided with brief reading selections and will be asked questions relating to the selections. All of the information required to answer the questions will be presented in the selections; the candidates will not be required to have any special knowledge relating to the content area covered in the selections.

2. <u>Spelling</u>
   These questions are designed to test the candidates' ability to spell words that office employees encounter in their daily work. Each question will consist of three sentences, each containing an underlined word. The candidates are to indicate which one, if any, of the underlined words are misspelled. If all are correct, the candidates should choose the "None is misspelled" response.

3. <u>English Grammar and Usage; Punctuation</u>
   The English grammar and usage questions are designed to test the candidates' ability to apply the basic rules of English grammar, usage, and sentence structure. The punctuation questions are designed to test the candidates' knowledge of appropriate punctuation marks and their correct placement in sentences.

4. <u>Keyboarding Practices</u>
   These questions are designed to test the candidates' knowledge of preferred practices in areas such as, but not limited to, capitalization, hyphenation, spacing, word division, tabulation and proofreading.

The passing score for the written examination will be determined at a date following the administration of the examination.

HOW TO TAKE A TEST

I. YOU MUST PASS AN EXAMINATION

A. *WHAT EVERY CANDIDATE SHOULD KNOW*

Examination applicants often ask us for help in preparing for the written test. What can I study in advance? What kinds of questions will be asked? How will the test be given? How will the papers be graded?

As an applicant for a civil service examination, you may be wondering about some of these things. Our purpose here is to suggest effective methods of advance study and to describe civil service examinations.

Your chances for success on this examination can be increased if you know how to prepare. Those "pre-examination jitters" can be reduced if you know what to expect. You can even experience an adventure in good citizenship if you know why civil service exams are given.

B. *WHY ARE CIVIL SERVICE EXAMINATIONS GIVEN?*

Civil service examinations are important to you in two ways. As a citizen, you want public jobs filled by employees who know how to do their work. As a job seeker, you want a fair chance to compete for that job on an equal footing with other candidates. The best-known means of accomplishing this two-fold goal is the competitive examination.

Exams are widely publicized throughout the nation. They may be administered for jobs in federal, state, city, municipal, town or village governments or agencies.

Any citizen may apply, with some limitations, such as the age or residence of applicants. Your experience and education may be reviewed to see whether you meet the requirements for the particular examination. When these requirements exist, they are reasonable and applied consistently to all applicants. Thus, a competitive examination may cause you some uneasiness now, but it is your privilege and safeguard.

C. *HOW ARE CIVIL SERVICE EXAMS DEVELOPED?*

Examinations are carefully written by trained technicians who are specialists in the field known as "psychological measurement," in consultation with recognized authorities in the field of work that the test will cover. These experts recommend the subject matter areas or skills to be tested; only those knowledges or skills important to your success on the job are included. The most reliable books and source materials available are used as references. Together, the experts and technicians judge the difficulty level of the questions.

Test technicians know how to phrase questions so that the problem is clearly stated. Their ethics do not permit "trick" or "catch" questions. Questions may have been tried out on sample groups, or subjected to statistical analysis, to determine their usefulness.

Written tests are often used in combination with performance tests, ratings of training and experience, and oral interviews. All of these measures combine to form the best-known means of finding the right person for the right job.

II. HOW TO PASS THE WRITTEN TEST

A. NATURE OF THE EXAMINATION

To prepare intelligently for civil service examinations, you should know how they differ from school examinations you have taken. In school you were assigned certain definite pages to read or subjects to cover. The examination questions were quite detailed and usually emphasized memory. Civil service exams, on the other hand, try to discover your present ability to perform the duties of a position, plus your potentiality to learn these duties. In other words, a civil service exam attempts to predict how successful you will be. Questions cover such a broad area that they cannot be as minute and detailed as school exam questions.

In the public service similar kinds of work, or positions, are grouped together in one "class." This process is known as *position-classification*. All the positions in a class are paid according to the salary range for that class. One class title covers all of these positions, and they are all tested by the same examination.

B. FOUR BASIC STEPS

1) Study the announcement

How, then, can you know what subjects to study? Our best answer is: "Learn as much as possible about the class of positions for which you've applied." The exam will test the knowledge, skills and abilities needed to do the work.

Your most valuable source of information about the position you want is the official exam announcement. This announcement lists the training and experience qualifications. Check these standards and apply only if you come reasonably close to meeting them.

The brief description of the position in the examination announcement offers some clues to the subjects which will be tested. Think about the job itself. Review the duties in your mind. Can you perform them, or are there some in which you are rusty? Fill in the blank spots in your preparation.

Many jurisdictions preview the written test in the exam announcement by including a section called "Knowledge and Abilities Required," "Scope of the Examination," or some similar heading. Here you will find out specifically what fields will be tested.

2) Review your own background

Once you learn in general what the position is all about, and what you need to know to do the work, ask yourself which subjects you already know fairly well and which need improvement. You may wonder whether to concentrate on improving your strong areas or on building some background in your fields of weakness. When the announcement has specified "some knowledge" or "considerable knowledge," or has used adjectives like "beginning principles of..." or "advanced ... methods," you can get a clue as to the number and difficulty of questions to be asked in any given field. More questions, and hence broader coverage, would be included for those subjects which are more important in the work. Now weigh your strengths and weaknesses against the job requirements and prepare accordingly.

3) Determine the level of the position

Another way to tell how intensively you should prepare is to understand the level of the job for which you are applying. Is it the entering level? In other words, is this the position in which beginners in a field of work are hired? Or is it an intermediate or advanced level? Sometimes this is indicated by such words as "Junior" or "Senior" in the class title. Other jurisdictions use Roman numerals to designate the level – Clerk I, Clerk II, for example. The word "Supervisor" sometimes appears in the title. If the level is not indicated by the title, check the description of duties. Will you be working under very close supervision, or will you have responsibility for independent decisions in this work?

4) Choose appropriate study materials

Now that you know the subjects to be examined and the relative amount of each subject to be covered, you can choose suitable study materials. For beginning level jobs, or even advanced ones, if you have a pronounced weakness in some aspect of your training, read a modern, standard textbook in that field. Be sure it is up to date and has general coverage. Such books are normally available at your library, and the librarian will be glad to help you locate one. For entry-level positions, questions of appropriate difficulty are chosen – neither highly advanced questions, nor those too simple. Such questions require careful thought but not advanced training.

If the position for which you are applying is technical or advanced, you will read more advanced, specialized material. If you are already familiar with the basic principles of your field, elementary textbooks would waste your time. Concentrate on advanced textbooks and technical periodicals. Think through the concepts and review difficult problems in your field.

These are all general sources. You can get more ideas on your own initiative, following these leads. For example, training manuals and publications of the government agency which employs workers in your field can be useful, particularly for technical and professional positions. A letter or visit to the government department involved may result in more specific study suggestions, and certainly will provide you with a more definite idea of the exact nature of the position you are seeking.

III. KINDS OF TESTS

Tests are used for purposes other than measuring knowledge and ability to perform specified duties. For some positions, it is equally important to test ability to make adjustments to new situations or to profit from training. In others, basic mental abilities not dependent on information are essential. Questions which test these things may not appear as pertinent to the duties of the position as those which test for knowledge and information. Yet they are often highly important parts of a fair examination. For very general questions, it is almost impossible to help you direct your study efforts. What we can do is to point out some of the more common of these general abilities needed in public service positions and describe some typical questions.

1) General information

Broad, general information has been found useful for predicting job success in some kinds of work. This is tested in a variety of ways, from vocabulary lists to questions about current events. Basic background in some field of work, such as sociology or economics, may be sampled in a group of questions. Often these are principles which have become familiar to most persons through exposure rather than through formal training. It is difficult to advise you how to study for these questions; being alert to the world around you is our best suggestion.

2) Verbal ability

An example of an ability needed in many positions is verbal or language ability. Verbal ability is, in brief, the ability to use and understand words. Vocabulary and grammar tests are typical measures of this ability. Reading comprehension or paragraph interpretation questions are common in many kinds of civil service tests. You are given a paragraph of written material and asked to find its central meaning.

3) Numerical ability

Number skills can be tested by the familiar arithmetic problem, by checking paired lists of numbers to see which are alike and which are different, or by interpreting charts and graphs. In the latter test, a graph may be printed in the test booklet which you are asked to use as the basis for answering questions.

4) Observation

A popular test for law-enforcement positions is the observation test. A picture is shown to you for several minutes, then taken away. Questions about the picture test your ability to observe both details and larger elements.

5) Following directions

In many positions in the public service, the employee must be able to carry out written instructions dependably and accurately. You may be given a chart with several columns, each column listing a variety of information. The questions require you to carry out directions involving the information given in the chart.

6) Skills and aptitudes

Performance tests effectively measure some manual skills and aptitudes. When the skill is one in which you are trained, such as typing or shorthand, you can practice. These tests are often very much like those given in business school or high school courses. For many of the other skills and aptitudes, however, no short-time preparation can be made. Skills and abilities natural to you or that you have developed throughout your lifetime are being tested.

Many of the general questions just described provide all the data needed to answer the questions and ask you to use your reasoning ability to find the answers. Your best preparation for these tests, as well as for tests of facts and ideas, is to be at your physical and mental best. You, no doubt, have your own methods of getting into an exam-taking mood and keeping "in shape." The next section lists some ideas on this subject.

IV. KINDS OF QUESTIONS

Only rarely is the "essay" question, which you answer in narrative form, used in civil service tests. Civil service tests are usually of the short-answer type. Full instructions for answering these questions will be given to you at the examination. But in case this is your first experience with short-answer questions and separate answer sheets, here is what you need to know:

1) **Multiple-choice Questions**

Most popular of the short-answer questions is the "multiple choice" or "best answer" question. It can be used, for example, to test for factual knowledge, ability to solve problems or judgment in meeting situations found at work.

A multiple-choice question is normally one of three types—
- It can begin with an incomplete statement followed by several possible endings. You are to find the one ending which *best* completes the statement, although some of the others may not be entirely wrong.
- It can also be a complete statement in the form of a question which is answered by choosing one of the statements listed.

- It can be in the form of a problem – again you select the best answer.

Here is an example of a multiple-choice question with a discussion which should give you some clues as to the method for choosing the right answer:

When an employee has a complaint about his assignment, the action which will *best* help him overcome his difficulty is to
  A. discuss his difficulty with his coworkers
  B. take the problem to the head of the organization
  C. take the problem to the person who gave him the assignment
  D. say nothing to anyone about his complaint

In answering this question, you should study each of the choices to find which is best. Consider choice "A" – Certainly an employee may discuss his complaint with fellow employees, but no change or improvement can result, and the complaint remains unresolved. Choice "B" is a poor choice since the head of the organization probably does not know what assignment you have been given, and taking your problem to him is known as "going over the head" of the supervisor. The supervisor, or person who made the assignment, is the person who can clarify it or correct any injustice. Choice "C" is, therefore, correct. To say nothing, as in choice "D," is unwise. Supervisors have and interest in knowing the problems employees are facing, and the employee is seeking a solution to his problem.

2) True/False Questions

The "true/false" or "right/wrong" form of question is sometimes used. Here a complete statement is given. Your job is to decide whether the statement is right or wrong.

SAMPLE: A roaming cell-phone call to a nearby city costs less than a non-roaming call to a distant city.

This statement is wrong, or false, since roaming calls are more expensive.

This is not a complete list of all possible question forms, although most of the others are variations of these common types. You will always get complete directions for answering questions. Be sure you understand *how* to mark your answers – ask questions until you do.

V. RECORDING YOUR ANSWERS

Computer terminals are used more and more today for many different kinds of exams.

For an examination with very few applicants, you may be told to record your answers in the test booklet itself. Separate answer sheets are much more common. If this separate answer sheet is to be scored by machine – and this is often the case – it is highly important that you mark your answers correctly in order to get credit.

An electronic scoring machine is often used in civil service offices because of the speed with which papers can be scored. Machine-scored answer sheets must be marked with a pencil, which will be given to you. This pencil has a high graphite content which responds to the electronic scoring machine. As a matter of fact, stray dots may register as answers, so do not let your pencil rest on the answer sheet while you are pondering the correct answer. Also, if your pencil lead breaks or is otherwise defective, ask for another.

Since the answer sheet will be dropped in a slot in the scoring machine, be careful not to bend the corners or get the paper crumpled.

The answer sheet normally has five vertical columns of numbers, with 30 numbers to a column. These numbers correspond to the question numbers in your test booklet. After each number, going across the page are four or five pairs of dotted lines. These short dotted lines have small letters or numbers above them. The first two pairs may also have a "T" or "F" above the letters. This indicates that the first two pairs only are to be used if the questions are of the true-false type. If the questions are multiple choice, disregard the "T" and "F" and pay attention only to the small letters or numbers.

Answer your questions in the manner of the sample that follows:

32. The largest city in the United States is
    A. Washington, D.C.
    B. New York City
    C. Chicago
    D. Detroit
    E. San Francisco

1) Choose the answer you think is best. (New York City is the largest, so "B" is correct.)
2) Find the row of dotted lines numbered the same as the question you are answering. (Find row number 32)
3) Find the pair of dotted lines corresponding to the answer. (Find the pair of lines under the mark "B.")
4) Make a solid black mark between the dotted lines.

VI. BEFORE THE TEST

Common sense will help you find procedures to follow to get ready for an examination. Too many of us, however, overlook these sensible measures. Indeed, nervousness and fatigue have been found to be the most serious reasons why applicants fail to do their best on civil service tests. Here is a list of reminders:

- Begin your preparation early – Don't wait until the last minute to go scurrying around for books and materials or to find out what the position is all about.
- Prepare continuously – An hour a night for a week is better than an all-night cram session. This has been definitely established. What is more, a night a week for a month will return better dividends than crowding your study into a shorter period of time.
- Locate the place of the exam – You have been sent a notice telling you when and where to report for the examination. If the location is in a different town or otherwise unfamiliar to you, it would be well to inquire the best route and learn something about the building.
- Relax the night before the test – Allow your mind to rest. Do not study at all that night. Plan some mild recreation or diversion; then go to bed early and get a good night's sleep.
- Get up early enough to make a leisurely trip to the place for the test – This way unforeseen events, traffic snarls, unfamiliar buildings, etc. will not upset you.
- Dress comfortably – A written test is not a fashion show. You will be known by number and not by name, so wear something comfortable.

- Leave excess paraphernalia at home – Shopping bags and odd bundles will get in your way. You need bring only the items mentioned in the official notice you received; usually everything you need is provided. Do not bring reference books to the exam. They will only confuse those last minutes and be taken away from you when in the test room.
- Arrive somewhat ahead of time – If because of transportation schedules you must get there very early, bring a newspaper or magazine to take your mind off yourself while waiting.
- Locate the examination room – When you have found the proper room, you will be directed to the seat or part of the room where you will sit. Sometimes you are given a sheet of instructions to read while you are waiting. Do not fill out any forms until you are told to do so; just read them and be prepared.
- Relax and prepare to listen to the instructions
- If you have any physical problem that may keep you from doing your best, be sure to tell the test administrator. If you are sick or in poor health, you really cannot do your best on the exam. You can come back and take the test some other time.

VII. AT THE TEST

The day of the test is here and you have the test booklet in your hand. The temptation to get going is very strong. Caution! There is more to success than knowing the right answers. You must know how to identify your papers and understand variations in the type of short-answer question used in this particular examination. Follow these suggestions for maximum results from your efforts:

1) Cooperate with the monitor

The test administrator has a duty to create a situation in which you can be as much at ease as possible. He will give instructions, tell you when to begin, check to see that you are marking your answer sheet correctly, and so on. He is not there to guard you, although he will see that your competitors do not take unfair advantage. He wants to help you do your best.

2) Listen to all instructions

Don't jump the gun! Wait until you understand all directions. In most civil service tests you get more time than you need to answer the questions. So don't be in a hurry. Read each word of instructions until you clearly understand the meaning. Study the examples, listen to all announcements and follow directions. Ask questions if you do not understand what to do.

3) Identify your papers

Civil service exams are usually identified by number only. You will be assigned a number; you must not put your name on your test papers. Be sure to copy your number correctly. Since more than one exam may be given, copy your exact examination title.

4) Plan your time

Unless you are told that a test is a "speed" or "rate of work" test, speed itself is usually not important. Time enough to answer all the questions will be provided, but this does not mean that you have all day. An overall time limit has been set. Divide the total time (in minutes) by the number of questions to determine the approximate time you have for each question.

5) Do not linger over difficult questions

If you come across a difficult question, mark it with a paper clip (useful to have along) and come back to it when you have been through the booklet. One caution if you do this – be sure to skip a number on your answer sheet as well. Check often to be sure that you have not lost your place and that you are marking in the row numbered the same as the question you are answering.

6) Read the questions

Be sure you know what the question asks! Many capable people are unsuccessful because they failed to *read* the questions correctly.

7) Answer all questions

Unless you have been instructed that a penalty will be deducted for incorrect answers, it is better to guess than to omit a question.

8) Speed tests

It is often better NOT to guess on speed tests. It has been found that on timed tests people are tempted to spend the last few seconds before time is called in marking answers at random – without even reading them – in the hope of picking up a few extra points. To discourage this practice, the instructions may warn you that your score will be "corrected" for guessing. That is, a penalty will be applied. The incorrect answers will be deducted from the correct ones, or some other penalty formula will be used.

9) Review your answers

If you finish before time is called, go back to the questions you guessed or omitted to give them further thought. Review other answers if you have time.

10) Return your test materials

If you are ready to leave before others have finished or time is called, take ALL your materials to the monitor and leave quietly. Never take any test material with you. The monitor can discover whose papers are not complete, and taking a test booklet may be grounds for disqualification.

VIII. EXAMINATION TECHNIQUES

1) Read the general instructions carefully. These are usually printed on the first page of the exam booklet. As a rule, these instructions refer to the timing of the examination; the fact that you should not start work until the signal and must stop work at a signal, etc. If there are any *special* instructions, such as a choice of questions to be answered, make sure that you note this instruction carefully.

2) When you are ready to start work on the examination, that is as soon as the signal has been given, read the instructions to each question booklet, underline any key words or phrases, such as *least, best, outline, describe* and the like. In this way you will tend to answer as requested rather than discover on reviewing your paper that you *listed without describing*, that you selected the *worst* choice rather than the *best* choice, etc.

3) If the examination is of the objective or multiple-choice type – that is, each question will also give a series of possible answers: A, B, C or D, and you are called upon to select the best answer and write the letter next to that answer on your answer paper – it is advisable to start answering each question in turn. There may be anywhere from 50 to 100 such questions in the three or four hours allotted and you can see how much time would be taken if you read through all the questions before beginning to answer any. Furthermore, if you come across a question or group of questions which you know would be difficult to answer, it would undoubtedly affect your handling of all the other questions.

4) If the examination is of the essay type and contains but a few questions, it is a moot point as to whether you should read all the questions before starting to answer any one. Of course, if you are given a choice – say five out of seven and the like – then it is essential to read all the questions so you can eliminate the two that are most difficult. If, however, you are asked to answer all the questions, there may be danger in trying to answer the easiest one first because you may find that you will spend too much time on it. The best technique is to answer the first question, then proceed to the second, etc.

5) Time your answers. Before the exam begins, write down the time it started, then add the time allowed for the examination and write down the time it must be completed, then divide the time available somewhat as follows:
    - If 3-1/2 hours are allowed, that would be 210 minutes. If you have 80 objective-type questions, that would be an average of 2-1/2 minutes per question. Allow yourself no more than 2 minutes per question, or a total of 160 minutes, which will permit about 50 minutes to review.
    - If for the time allotment of 210 minutes there are 7 essay questions to answer, that would average about 30 minutes a question. Give yourself only 25 minutes per question so that you have about 35 minutes to review.

6) The most important instruction is to *read each question* and make sure you know what is wanted. The second most important instruction is to *time yourself properly* so that you answer every question. The third most important instruction is to *answer every question*. Guess if you have to but include something for each question. Remember that you will receive no credit for a blank and will probably receive some credit if you write something in answer to an essay question. If you guess a letter – say "B" for a multiple-choice question – you may have guessed right. If you leave a blank as an answer to a multiple-choice question, the examiners may respect your feelings but it will not add a point to your score. Some exams may penalize you for wrong answers, so in such cases *only*, you may not want to guess unless you have some basis for your answer.

7) Suggestions
    a. Objective-type questions
        1. Examine the question booklet for proper sequence of pages and questions
        2. Read all instructions carefully
        3. Skip any question which seems too difficult; return to it after all other questions have been answered
        4. Apportion your time properly; do not spend too much time on any single question or group of questions

5. Note and underline key words – *all, most, fewest, least, best, worst, same, opposite*, etc.
   6. Pay particular attention to negatives
   7. Note unusual option, e.g., unduly long, short, complex, different or similar in content to the body of the question
   8. Observe the use of "hedging" words – *probably, may, most likely*, etc.
   9. Make sure that your answer is put next to the same number as the question
   10. Do not second-guess unless you have good reason to believe the second answer is definitely more correct
   11. Cross out original answer if you decide another answer is more accurate; do not erase until you are ready to hand your paper in
   12. Answer all questions; guess unless instructed otherwise
   13. Leave time for review

   b. Essay questions
      1. Read each question carefully
      2. Determine exactly what is wanted. Underline key words or phrases.
      3. Decide on outline or paragraph answer
      4. Include many different points and elements unless asked to develop any one or two points or elements
      5. Show impartiality by giving pros and cons unless directed to select one side only
      6. Make and write down any assumptions you find necessary to answer the questions
      7. Watch your English, grammar, punctuation and choice of words
      8. Time your answers; don't crowd material

8) Answering the essay question

Most essay questions can be answered by framing the specific response around several key words or ideas. Here are a few such key words or ideas:

M's: manpower, materials, methods, money, management
P's: purpose, program, policy, plan, procedure, practice, problems, pitfalls, personnel, public relations

   a. Six basic steps in handling problems:
      1. Preliminary plan and background development
      2. Collect information, data and facts
      3. Analyze and interpret information, data and facts
      4. Analyze and develop solutions as well as make recommendations
      5. Prepare report and sell recommendations
      6. Install recommendations and follow up effectiveness

   b. Pitfalls to avoid
      1. *Taking things for granted* – A statement of the situation does not necessarily imply that each of the elements is necessarily true; for example, a complaint may be invalid and biased so that all that can be taken for granted is that a complaint has been registered

2. *Considering only one side of a situation* – Wherever possible, indicate several alternatives and then point out the reasons you selected the best one
3. *Failing to indicate follow up* – Whenever your answer indicates action on your part, make certain that you will take proper follow-up action to see how successful your recommendations, procedures or actions turn out to be
4. *Taking too long in answering any single question* – Remember to time your answers properly

IX. AFTER THE TEST

Scoring procedures differ in detail among civil service jurisdictions although the general principles are the same. Whether the papers are hand-scored or graded by machine we have described, they are nearly always graded by number. That is, the person who marks the paper knows only the number – never the name – of the applicant. Not until all the papers have been graded will they be matched with names. If other tests, such as training and experience or oral interview ratings have been given, scores will be combined. Different parts of the examination usually have different weights. For example, the written test might count 60 percent of the final grade, and a rating of training and experience 40 percent. In many jurisdictions, veterans will have a certain number of points added to their grades.

After the final grade has been determined, the names are placed in grade order and an eligible list is established. There are various methods for resolving ties between those who get the same final grade – probably the most common is to place first the name of the person whose application was received first. Job offers are made from the eligible list in the order the names appear on it. You will be notified of your grade and your rank as soon as all these computations have been made. This will be done as rapidly as possible.

People who are found to meet the requirements in the announcement are called "eligibles." Their names are put on a list of eligible candidates. An eligible's chances of getting a job depend on how high he stands on this list and how fast agencies are filling jobs from the list.

When a job is to be filled from a list of eligibles, the agency asks for the names of people on the list of eligibles for that job. When the civil service commission receives this request, it sends to the agency the names of the three people highest on this list. Or, if the job to be filled has specialized requirements, the office sends the agency the names of the top three persons who meet these requirements from the general list.

The appointing officer makes a choice from among the three people whose names were sent to him. If the selected person accepts the appointment, the names of the others are put back on the list to be considered for future openings.

That is the rule in hiring from all kinds of eligible lists, whether they are for typist, carpenter, chemist, or something else. For every vacancy, the appointing officer has his choice of any one of the top three eligibles on the list. This explains why the person whose name is on top of the list sometimes does not get an appointment when some of the persons lower on the list do. If the appointing officer chooses the second or third eligible, the No. 1 eligible does not get a job at once, but stays on the list until he is appointed or the list is terminated.

X. HOW TO PASS THE INTERVIEW TEST

The examination for which you applied requires an oral interview test. You have already taken the written test and you are now being called for the interview test – the final part of the formal examination.

You may think that it is not possible to prepare for an interview test and that there are no procedures to follow during an interview. Our purpose is to point out some things you can do in advance that will help you and some good rules to follow and pitfalls to avoid while you are being interviewed.

What is an interview supposed to test?

The written examination is designed to test the technical knowledge and competence of the candidate; the oral is designed to evaluate intangible qualities, not readily measured otherwise, and to establish a list showing the relative fitness of each candidate – as measured against his competitors – for the position sought. Scoring is not on the basis of "right" and "wrong," but on a sliding scale of values ranging from "not passable" to "outstanding." As a matter of fact, it is possible to achieve a relatively low score without a single "incorrect" answer because of evident weakness in the qualities being measured.

Occasionally, an examination may consist entirely of an oral test – either an individual or a group oral. In such cases, information is sought concerning the technical knowledges and abilities of the candidate, since there has been no written examination for this purpose. More commonly, however, an oral test is used to supplement a written examination.

Who conducts interviews?

The composition of oral boards varies among different jurisdictions. In nearly all, a representative of the personnel department serves as chairman. One of the members of the board may be a representative of the department in which the candidate would work. In some cases, "outside experts" are used, and, frequently, a businessman or some other representative of the general public is asked to serve. Labor and management or other special groups may be represented. The aim is to secure the services of experts in the appropriate field.

However the board is composed, it is a good idea (and not at all improper or unethical) to ascertain in advance of the interview who the members are and what groups they represent. When you are introduced to them, you will have some idea of their backgrounds and interests, and at least you will not stutter and stammer over their names.

What should be done before the interview?

While knowledge about the board members is useful and takes some of the surprise element out of the interview, there is other preparation which is more substantive. It *is* possible to prepare for an oral interview – in several ways:

1) Keep a copy of your application and review it carefully before the interview

This may be the only document before the oral board, and the starting point of the interview. Know what education and experience you have listed there, and the sequence and dates of all of it. Sometimes the board will ask you to review the highlights of your experience for them; you should not have to hem and haw doing it.

2) Study the class specification and the examination announcement

Usually, the oral board has one or both of these to guide them. The qualities, characteristics or knowledges required by the position sought are stated in these documents. They offer valuable clues as to the nature of the oral interview. For example, if the job involves supervisory responsibilities, the announcement will usually indicate that knowledge of modern supervisory methods and the qualifications of the candidate as a supervisor will be tested. If so, you can expect such questions, frequently in the form of a hypothetical situation which you are expected to solve. NEVER go into an oral without knowledge of the duties and responsibilities of the job you seek.

3) Think through each qualification required

Try to visualize the kind of questions you would ask if you were a board member. How well could you answer them? Try especially to appraise your own knowledge and background in each area, *measured against the job sought*, and identify any areas in which you are weak. Be critical and realistic – do not flatter yourself.

4) Do some general reading in areas in which you feel you may be weak

For example, if the job involves supervision and your past experience has NOT, some general reading in supervisory methods and practices, particularly in the field of human relations, might be useful. Do NOT study agency procedures or detailed manuals. The oral board will be testing your understanding and capacity, not your memory.

5) Get a good night's sleep and watch your general health and mental attitude

You will want a clear head at the interview. Take care of a cold or any other minor ailment, and of course, no hangovers.

What should be done on the day of the interview?

Now comes the day of the interview itself. Give yourself plenty of time to get there. Plan to arrive somewhat ahead of the scheduled time, particularly if your appointment is in the fore part of the day. If a previous candidate fails to appear, the board might be ready for you a bit early. By early afternoon an oral board is almost invariably behind schedule if there are many candidates, and you may have to wait. Take along a book or magazine to read, or your application to review, but leave any extraneous material in the waiting room when you go in for your interview. In any event, relax and compose yourself.

The matter of dress is important. The board is forming impressions about you – from your experience, your manners, your attitude, and your appearance. Give your personal appearance careful attention. Dress your best, but not your flashiest. Choose conservative, appropriate clothing, and be sure it is immaculate. This is a business interview, and your appearance should indicate that you regard it as such. Besides, being well groomed and properly dressed will help boost your confidence.

Sooner or later, someone will call your name and escort you into the interview room. *This is it.* From here on you are on your own. It is too late for any more preparation. But remember, you asked for this opportunity to prove your fitness, and you are here because your request was granted.

What happens when you go in?

The usual sequence of events will be as follows: The clerk (who is often the board stenographer) will introduce you to the chairman of the oral board, who will introduce you to the other members of the board. Acknowledge the introductions before you sit down. Do not be surprised if you find a microphone facing you or a stenotypist sitting by. Oral interviews are usually recorded in the event of an appeal or other review.

Usually the chairman of the board will open the interview by reviewing the highlights of your education and work experience from your application – primarily for the benefit of the other members of the board, as well as to get the material into the record. Do not interrupt or comment unless there is an error or significant misinterpretation; if that is the case, do not hesitate. But do not quibble about insignificant matters. Also, he will usually ask you some question about your education, experience or your present job – partly to get you to start talking and to establish the interviewing "rapport." He may start the actual questioning, or turn it over to one of the other members. Frequently, each member undertakes the questioning on a particular area, one in which he is perhaps most competent, so you can expect each member to participate in the examination. Because time is limited, you may also expect some rather abrupt switches in the direction the questioning takes, so do not be upset by it. Normally, a board member will not pursue a single line of questioning unless he discovers a particular strength or weakness.

After each member has participated, the chairman will usually ask whether any member has any further questions, then will ask you if you have anything you wish to add. Unless you are expecting this question, it may floor you. Worse, it may start you off on an extended, extemporaneous speech. The board is not usually seeking more information. The question is principally to offer you a last opportunity to present further qualifications or to indicate that you have nothing to add. So, if you feel that a significant qualification or characteristic has been overlooked, it is proper to point it out in a sentence or so. Do not compliment the board on the thoroughness of their examination – they have been sketchy, and you know it. If you wish, merely say, "No thank you, I have nothing further to add." This is a point where you can "talk yourself out" of a good impression or fail to present an important bit of information. Remember, *you close the interview yourself*.

The chairman will then say, "That is all, Mr. _____, thank you." Do not be startled; the interview is over, and quicker than you think. Thank him, gather your belongings and take your leave. Save your sigh of relief for the other side of the door.

How to put your best foot forward

Throughout this entire process, you may feel that the board individually and collectively is trying to pierce your defenses, seek out your hidden weaknesses and embarrass and confuse you. Actually, this is not true. They are obliged to make an appraisal of your qualifications for the job you are seeking, and they want to see you in your best light. Remember, they must interview all candidates and a non-cooperative candidate may become a failure in spite of their best efforts to bring out his qualifications. Here are 15 suggestions that will help you:

1) Be natural – Keep your attitude confident, not cocky

If you are not confident that you can do the job, do not expect the board to be. Do not apologize for your weaknesses, try to bring out your strong points. The board is interested in a positive, not negative, presentation. Cockiness will antagonize any board member and make him wonder if you are covering up a weakness by a false show of strength.

2) Get comfortable, but don't lounge or sprawl

Sit erectly but not stiffly. A careless posture may lead the board to conclude that you are careless in other things, or at least that you are not impressed by the importance of the occasion. Either conclusion is natural, even if incorrect. Do not fuss with your clothing, a pencil or an ashtray. Your hands may occasionally be useful to emphasize a point; do not let them become a point of distraction.

3) Do not wisecrack or make small talk

This is a serious situation, and your attitude should show that you consider it as such. Further, the time of the board is limited – they do not want to waste it, and neither should you.

4) Do not exaggerate your experience or abilities

In the first place, from information in the application or other interviews and sources, the board may know more about you than you think. Secondly, you probably will not get away with it. An experienced board is rather adept at spotting such a situation, so do not take the chance.

5) If you know a board member, do not make a point of it, yet do not hide it

Certainly you are not fooling him, and probably not the other members of the board. Do not try to take advantage of your acquaintanceship – it will probably do you little good.

6) Do not dominate the interview

Let the board do that. They will give you the clues – do not assume that you have to do all the talking. Realize that the board has a number of questions to ask you, and do not try to take up all the interview time by showing off your extensive knowledge of the answer to the first one.

7) Be attentive

You only have 20 minutes or so, and you should keep your attention at its sharpest throughout. When a member is addressing a problem or question to you, give him your undivided attention. Address your reply principally to him, but do not exclude the other board members.

8) Do not interrupt

A board member may be stating a problem for you to analyze. He will ask you a question when the time comes. Let him state the problem, and wait for the question.

9) Make sure you understand the question

Do not try to answer until you are sure what the question is. If it is not clear, restate it in your own words or ask the board member to clarify it for you. However, do not haggle about minor elements.

10) Reply promptly but not hastily

A common entry on oral board rating sheets is "candidate responded readily," or "candidate hesitated in replies." Respond as promptly and quickly as you can, but do not jump to a hasty, ill-considered answer.

11) Do not be peremptory in your answers

A brief answer is proper – but do not fire your answer back. That is a losing game from your point of view. The board member can probably ask questions much faster than you can answer them.

12) Do not try to create the answer you think the board member wants

He is interested in what kind of mind you have and how it works – not in playing games. Furthermore, he can usually spot this practice and will actually grade you down on it.

13) Do not switch sides in your reply merely to agree with a board member

Frequently, a member will take a contrary position merely to draw you out and to see if you are willing and able to defend your point of view. Do not start a debate, yet do not surrender a good position. If a position is worth taking, it is worth defending.

14) Do not be afraid to admit an error in judgment if you are shown to be wrong

The board knows that you are forced to reply without any opportunity for careful consideration. Your answer may be demonstrably wrong. If so, admit it and get on with the interview.

15) Do not dwell at length on your present job

The opening question may relate to your present assignment. Answer the question but do not go into an extended discussion. You are being examined for a *new* job, not your present one. As a matter of fact, try to phrase ALL your answers in terms of the job for which you are being examined.

Basis of Rating

Probably you will forget most of these "do's" and "don'ts" when you walk into the oral interview room. Even remembering them all will not ensure you a passing grade. Perhaps you did not have the qualifications in the first place. But remembering them will help you to put your best foot forward, without treading on the toes of the board members.

Rumor and popular opinion to the contrary notwithstanding, an oral board wants you to make the best appearance possible. They know you are under pressure – but they also want to see how you respond to it as a guide to what your reaction would be under the pressures of the job you seek. They will be influenced by the degree of poise you display, the personal traits you show and the manner in which you respond.

ABOUT THIS BOOK

This book contains tests divided into Examination Sections. Go through each test, answering every question in the margin. We have also attached a sample answer sheet at the back of the book that can be removed and used. At the end of each test look at the answer key and check your answers. On the ones you got wrong, look at the right answer choice and learn. Do not fill in the answers first. Do not memorize the questions and answers, but understand the answer and principles involved. On your test, the questions will likely be different from the samples. Questions are changed and new ones added. If you understand these past questions you should have success with any changes that arise. Tests may consist of several types of questions. We have additional books on each subject should more study be advisable or necessary for you. Finally, the more you study, the better prepared you will be. This book is intended to be the last thing you study before you walk into the examination room. Prior study of relevant texts is also recommended. NLC publishes some of these in our Fundamental Series. Knowledge and good sense are important factors in passing your exam. Good luck also helps. So now study this Passbook, absorb the material contained within and take that knowledge into the examination. Then do your best to pass that exam.

EXAMINATION SECTION

EXAMINATION SECTION
TEST 1

DIRECTIONS: Each question or incomplete statement is followed by several suggested answers or completions. Select the one that BEST answers the question or completes the statement. *PRINT THE LETTER OF THE CORRECT ANSWER IN THE SPACE AT THE RIGHT.*

1. A coworker has e-mailed a file containing a spreadsheet for your review. Which of the following programs will open the file?

    A. Adobe Reader
    B. Microsoft Excel
    C. Microsoft PowerPoint
    D. Adobe Illustrator

    1._____

2. A report needs to be forwarded immediately to a supervisor in another office. Which of the following is the LEAST effective way of giving the supervisor the report?

    A. scanning the report and e-mailing the file
    B. faxing it to the supervisor's office
    C. uploading it to the office network and informing the supervisor
    D. waiting for the supervisor to come to your office and giving it to him/her then

    2._____

3. Suppose your supervisor is on the telephone in his office and an applicant arrives for a scheduled interview with him.
Of the following, the BEST procedure to follow ordinarily is to

    A. informally chat with the applicant in your office until your supervisor has finished his phone conversation
    B. escort him directly into your supervisor's office and have him wait for him there
    C. inform your supervisor of the applicant's arrival and try to make the applicant feel comfortable while waiting
    D. have him hang up his coat and tell him to go directly in to see your supervisor

    3._____

Questions 4-9.

DIRECTIONS: Questions 4 through 9 each consist of a sentence which may or may not be an example of good English usage. Consider grammar, punctuation, spelling, capitalization, awkwardness, etc. Examine each sentence, and then choose the correct statement about it from the four choices below it. If the English usage in the sentence given is better than any of the changes suggested in options B, C, or D, choose option A. Do not choose an option that will change the meaning of the sentence.

4. The report, along with the accompanying documents, were submitted for review.

    A. This is an example of acceptable writing.
    B. The words *were submitted* should be changed to *was submitted*.
    C. The word *accompanying* should be spelled *accompaning*.
    D. The comma after the word *report* should be taken out.

    4._____

1

5. If others must use your files, be certain that they understand how the system works, but insist that you do all the filing and refiling. 5.____
   - A. This is an example of acceptable writing.
   - B. There should be a period after the word *works*, and the word *but* should start a new sentence.
   - C. The words *filing* and *refiling* should be spelled *fileing* and *refileing*.
   - D. There should be a comma after the word *but*.

6. The appeal was not considered because of its late arrival. 6.____
   - A. This is an example of acceptable writing.
   - B. The word *its* should be changed to *it's*.
   - C. The word *its* should be changed to *the*.
   - D. The words *late arrival* should be changed to *arrival late*.

7. The letter must be read carefuly to determine under which subject it should be filed. 7.____
   - A. This is an example of acceptable writing.
   - B. The word *under* should be changed to *at*.
   - C. The word *determine* should be spelled *determin*.
   - D. The word *carefuly* should be spelled *carefully*.

8. He showed potential as an office manager, but he lacked skill in delegating work. 8.____
   - A. This is an example of acceptable writing.
   - B. The word *delegating* should be spelled *delagating*.
   - C. The word *potential* should be spelled *potencial*.
   - D. The words *lie lacked* should be changed to *was lacking*.

9. His supervisor told him that it would be all right to receive personal mail at the office. 9.____
   - A. This is an example of acceptable writing.
   - B. The words *all right* should be changed to *alright*.
   - C. The word *personal* should be spelled *personel*.
   - D. The word *mail* should be changed to *letters*.

Questions 10-13.

DIRECTIONS: Questions 10 through 13 are to be answered SOLELY on the basis of the information given in the following passage.

Typed pages can reflect the simplicity of modern art in a machine age. Lightness and evenness can be achieved by proper layout and balance of typed lines and white space. Instead of solid, cramped masses of uneven, crowded typing, there should be a pleasing balance up and down as well as horizontal.

To have real balance, your page must have a center. The eyes see the center of the sheet slightly above the real center. This is the way both you and the reader see it. Try imagining a line down the center of the page that divides the paper in equal halves. On either side of your paper, white space and blocks of typing need to be similar in size and shape. Although left and right margins should be equal, top and bottom margins need not be as exact. It looks better to hold a bottom border wider than a top margin, so that your typing rests upon a cushion of white space. To add interest to the appearance of the page, try making one paragraph between one-half and two-thirds the size of an adjacent paragraph.

Thus, by taking full advantage of your typewriter, the pages that you type will not only be accurate but will also be attractive.

10. It can be inferred from the passage that the BASIC importance of proper balancing on a typed page is that proper balancing   10.____

    A. makes a typed page a work of modern art
    B. provides exercise in proper positioning of a typewriter
    C. increases the amount of typed copy on the paper
    D. draws greater attention and interest to the page

11. A reader will tend to see the center of a typed page   11.____

    A. somewhat higher than the true center
    B. somewhat lower than the true center
    C. on either side of the true center
    D. about two-thirds of an inch above the true center

12. Which of the following suggestions is NOT given by the passage?   12.____

    A. Bottom margins may be wider than top borders.
    B. Keep all paragraphs approximately the same size.
    C. Divide your page with an imaginary line down the middle.
    D. Side margins should be equalized.

13. Of the following, the BEST title for this passage is: 13.____

    A. INCREASING THE ACCURACY OF THE TYPED PAGE
    B. DETERMINATION OF MARGINS FOR TYPED COPY
    C. LAYOUT AND BALANCE OF THE TYPED PAGE
    D. HOW TO TAKE FULL ADVANTAGE OF THE TYPEWRITER

14. In order to type addresses on a large number of envelopes MOST efficiently, you should   14.____

    A. insert another envelope into the typewriter before removing each typed envelope
    B. take each typed envelope out of the machine before starting the next envelope
    C. insert several envelopes into the machine at one time, keeping all top and bottom edges even
    D. insert several envelopes into the machine at one time, keeping the top edge of each envelope two inches below the top edge of the one beneath it

15. A senior typist has completed copying a statistical report from a rough draft. Of the following, the BEST way to be sure that her typing is correct is for the typist to   15.____

    A. fold the rough draft, line it up with the typed copy, compare one-half of the columns with the original, and have a co-worker compare the other half
    B. check each line of the report as it is typed and then have a co-worker check each line again after the entire report is finished

3

C. have a co-worker add each column and check the totals on the typed copy with the totals on the original
D. have a co-worker read aloud from the rough draft while the typist checks the typed copy and then have the typist read while the co-worker checks

16. In order to center a heading when typing a report, you should   16.____

    A. measure your typing paper with a ruler and begin the heading one-third of the way in from the left margin
    B. begin the heading at the point on the typewriter scale which is 50 minus the number of letters in the heading
    C. multiply the number of characters in the heading by two and begin the heading that number of spaces in from the left margin
    D. begin the heading at the point on the scale which is equal to the center point of your paper minus one-half the number of characters and spaces in the heading

17. Which of the following recommendations concerning the use of copy paper for making typewritten copies should NOT be followed?   17.____

    A. Copy papers should be checked for wrinkles before being used.
    B. Legal-size copy paper may be folded if it is too large to fit into a convenient drawer space.
    C. When several sheets of paper are being used, they should be fastened with a paper clip at the top after insertion in the typewriter.
    D. For making many copies, paper of the same weight and brightness should be used.

18. Assume that a new typist, Norma Garcia, has been assigned to work under your supervision and is reporting to work for the first time. You formally introduce Norma to her co-workers and suggest that a few of the other typists explain the office procedures and typing formats to her. The practice of instructing Norma in her duties in this manner is   18.____

    A. *good* because she will be made to feel at home
    B. *good* because she will learn more about routine office tasks from co-workers than from you
    C. *poor* because her co-workers will resent the extra work
    D. *poor* because you will not have enough control over her training

19. Suppose that Jean Brown, a typist, is typing a letter following the same format that she has always used. However, she notices that the other two typists in her office are also typing letters, but are using a different format. Jean is concerned that she might not have been informed of a change in format.   19.____
Of the following, the FIRST action that Jean should take is to

    A. seek advice from her supervisor as to which format to use
    B. ask the other typists whether she should use a new format for typing letters
    C. disregard the format that the other typists are using and continue to type in the format she had been using
    D. use the format that the other typists are using, assuming that it is a newly accepted method

20. Suppose that the new office to which you have been assigned has put up Christmas decorations, and a Christmas party is being planned by the city agency in which you work. However, nothing has been said about Christmas gifts.
    It would be CORRECT for you to assume that

    A. you are expected to give a gift to your supervisor
    B. your supervisor will give you a gift
    C. you are expected to give gifts only to your subordinates
    D. you will neither receive gifts nor will you be expected to give any

KEY (CORRECT ANSWERS)

1.	B	11.	A
2.	D	12.	B
3.	C	13.	C
4.	B	14.	A
5.	A	15.	D
6.	A	16.	D
7.	D	17.	B
8.	A	18.	D
9.	A	19.	A
10.	D	20.	D

TEST 2

DIRECTIONS: Each question or incomplete statement is followed by several suggested answers or completions. Select the one that BEST answers the question or completes the statement. *PRINT THE LETTER OF THE CORRECT ANSWER IN THE SPACE AT THE RIGHT.*

1. The supervisor you assist is under great pressure to meet certain target dates. He has scheduled an emergency meeting to take place in a few days, and he asks you to send out notices immediately. As you begin to prepare the notices, however, you realize he has scheduled the meeting for a Saturday, which is not a working day. Also, you sense that your supervisor is not in a good mood.
Which of the following is the MOST effective method of handling this situation?

   A. Change the meeting date to the first working day after that Saturday and send out the notices.
   B. Change the meeting date to a working day on which his calendar is clear and send out the notices.
   C. Point out to your supervisor that the date is a Saturday.
   D. Send out the notices as they are since you have received specific instructions.

1.____

Questions 2-7.

DIRECTIONS: Questions 2 through 7 each consist of a sentence which may or may not be an example of good English usage. Consider grammar, punctuation, spelling, capitalization, awkwardness, etc. Examine each sentence, and then choose the correct statement about it from the four choices below it. If the English usage in the sentence given is better than any of the changes suggested in options B, C, or D, choose option A. Do not choose an option that will change the meaning of the sentence.

2. The typist used an extention cord in order to connect her typewriter to the outlet nearest to her desk.

   A. This is an example of acceptable writing.
   B. A period should be placed after the word *cord,* and the word *in* should have a capital I.
   C. A comma should be placed after the word *typewriter.*
   D. The word *extention* should be spelled *extension.*

2.____

3. He would have went to the conference if he had received an invitation.

   A. This is an example of acceptable writing.
   B. The word *went* should be replaced by the word *gone.*
   C. The word *had* should be replaced by *would have.*
   D. The word *conference* should be spelled *conferance.*

3.____

4. In order to make the report neater, he spent many hours rewriting it.

   A. This is an example of acceptable writing.
   B. The word *more* should be inserted before the word *neater.*
   C. There should be a colon after the word *neater.*
   D. The word *spent* should be changed to *have spent.*

4.____

5. His supervisor told him that he should of read the memorandum more carefully. 5.____

   A. This is an example of acceptable writing.
   B. The word *memorandum* should be spelled *memorandom*.
   C. The word *of* should be replaced by the word *have*.
   D. The word *carefully* should be replaced by the word *careful*.

6. It was decided that two separate reports should be written. 6.____

   A. This is an example of acceptable writing.
   B. A comma should be inserted after the word *decided*.
   C. The word *be* should be replaced by the word *been*.
   D. A colon should be inserted after the word *that*.

7. She don't seem to understand that the work must be done as soon as possible. 7.____

   A. This is an example of acceptable writing.
   B. The word *doesn't* should replace the word *don't*.
   C. The word *why* should replace the word *that*.
   D. The word *as* before the word *soon* should be eliminated.

Questions 8-11.

DIRECTIONS: Questions 8 through 11 are to be answered SOLELY on the basis of the following passage.

There is nothing that will take the place of good sense on the part of the stenographer. You may be perfect in transcribing exactly what the dictator says and your speed may be adequate; but without an understanding of the dictator's intent as well as his words, you are likely to be a mediocre secretary.

A serious error that is made when taking dictation is putting down something that does not make sense. Most people who dictate material would rather be asked to repeat and explain than to receive transcribed material which has errors due to inattention or doubt. Many dictators request that their grammar be corrected by their secretaries; but unless specifically asked to do so, secretaries should not do it without first checking with the dictator. Secretaries should be aware that, in some cases, dictators may use incorrect grammar or slang expressions to create a particular effect.

Some people dictate commas, periods, and paragraphs, while others expect the stenographer to know when, where, and how to punctuate. A well-trained secretary should be able to indicate the proper punctuation by listening to the pauses and tones of the dictator's voice.

A stenographer who has taken dictation from the same person for a period of time should be able to understand him under most conditions. By increasing her tact, alertness, and efficiency, a secretary can become more competent.

8. According to the passage, which of the following statements concerning the dictation of punctuation is CORRECT? 8.____
   A

   A. dictator may use incorrect punctuation to create a desired style

B. dictator should indicate all punctuation
C. stenographer should know how to punctuate based on the pauses and tones of the dictator
D. stenographer should not type any punctuation if it has not been dictated to her

9. According to the passage, how should secretaries handle grammatical errors in a dictation?
Secretaries should

   A. *not correct* grammatical errors unless the dictator is aware that this is being done
   B. *correct* grammatical errors by having the dictator repeat the line with proper pauses
   C. *correct* grammatical errors if they have checked the correctness in a grammar book
   D. *correct* grammatical errors based on their own good sense

10. If a stenographer is confused about the method of spacing and indenting of a report which has just been dictated to her, she GENERALLY should

    A. do the best she can
    B. ask the dictator to explain what she should do
    C. try to improve her ability to understand dictated material
    D. accept the fact that her stenographic ability is not adequate

11. In the last line of the first paragraph, the word *mediocre* means MOST NEARLY

    A. superior   B. disregarded
    C. respected   D. second-rate

12. Assume that is is your responsibility to schedule meetings for your supervisor, who believes in starting these meetings strictly on time. He has told you to schedule separate meetings with Mr. Smith and Ms. Jones, which will last approximately 20 minutes each. You have told Mr. Smith to arrive at 10:00 A.M. and Ms. Jones at 10:30 A.M. Your supervisor will have an hour of free time at 11:00 A.M. At 10:25 A.M., Mr. Smith arrives and states that there was a train delay, and he is sorry that he is late. Ms. Jones has not yet arrived. You do not know who Mr. Smith and Ms. Jones are or what the meetings will be about.
Of the following, the BEST course of action for you to take is to

    A. send Mr. Smith in to see your supervisor; and when Ms. Jones arrives, tell her that your supervisor's first meeting will take more time than he expected
    B. tell Mr. Smith that your supervisor has a meeting at 10:30 A.M. and that you will have to reschedule his meeting for another day
    C. check with your supervisor to find out if he would prefer to see Mr. Smith immediately or at 11:00 A.M.
    D. encourage your supervisor to meet with Mr. Smith immediately because Mr. Smith's late arrival was not intentional

13. Assume that you have been told by your boss not to let anyone disturb him for the rest of the afternoon unless absolutely necessary since he has to complete some urgent work. His supervisor, who is the bureau chief, telephones and asks to speak to him.
The BEST course of action for you to take is to

A. ask the bureau chief if he can leave a message
B. ask your boss if he can take the call
C. tell the bureau chief that your boss is out
D. tell your boss that his instructions will get you into trouble

14. Which one of the following is the MOST advisable procedure for a stenographer to follow when a dictator asks her to make extra copies of dictated material?

    A. Note the number of copies required at the beginning of the notes.
    B. Note the number of copies required at the end of the notes.
    C. Make a mental note of the number of copies required to be made.
    D. Make a checkmark beside the notes to serve as a reminder that extra copies are required.

15. Suppose that, as you are taking shorthand notes, the dictator tells you that the sentence he has just dictated is to be deleted.
    Of the following, the BEST thing for you to do is to

    A. place the correction in the left-hand margin next to the deleted sentence
    B. write the word *delete* over the sentence and place the correction on a separate page for corrections
    C. erase the sentence and use that available space for the correction
    D. draw a line through the sentence and begin the correction on the next available line

16. Assume that your supervisor, who normally dictates at a relatively slow rate, begins dictating to you very rapidly. You find it very difficult to keep up at this speed. Which one of the following is the BEST action to take in this situation?

    A. Ask your supervisor to dictate more slowly since you are having difficulty.
    B. Continue to take the dictation at the fast speed and fill in the blanks later.
    C. Interrupt your supervisor with a question about the dictation, hoping that when she begins again it will be slower.
    D. Refuse to take the dictation unless given at the speed indicated in your job description.

17. Assume that you have been asked to put a heading on the second, third, and fourth pages of a four-page letter to make sure they can be identified in case they are separated from the first page.
    Which of the following is it LEAST important to include in such a heading?

    A. Date of the letter
    B. Initials of the typist
    C. Name of the person to whom the letter is addressed
    D. Number of the page

18. Which one of the following is NOT generally accepted when dividing words at the end of a line?
    Dividing

    A. a hyphenated word at the hyphen
    B. a word immediately after the prefix
    C. a word immediately before the suffix
    D. proper names between syllables

19. In the preparation of a business letter which has two enclosures, the MOST generally accepted of the following procedures to follow is to type

   A. *See Attached Items* one line below the last line of the body of the letter
   B. *See Attached Enclosures* to the left of the signature
   C. *Enclosures 2* at the left margin below the signature line
   D. nothing on the letter to indicate enclosures since it will be obvious to the reader that there are enclosures in the envelope

20. Standard rules for typing spacing have developed through usage. According to these rules, one space is left AFTER

   A. a comma
   B. every sentence
   C. a colon
   D. an opening parenthesis

KEY (CORRECT ANSWERS)

1.	C	11.	D
2.	D	12.	C
3.	B	13.	B
4.	A	14.	A
5.	C	15.	D
6.	A	16.	A
7.	B	17.	B
8.	C	18.	D
9.	A	19.	C
10.	B	20.	A

EXAMINATION SECTION
TEST 1

DIRECTIONS: Each question or incomplete statement is followed by several suggested answers or completions. Select the one that BEST answers the question or completes the statement. *PRINT THE LETTER OF THE CORRECT ANSWER IN THE SPACE AT THE RIGHT.*

1. The ʌ or caret symbol is a proofreader's mark which means that a
   A. space should have been left between two words
   B. new paragraph should be indicated
   C. word, phrase, or punctuation mark should be inserted
   D. word that is abbreviated should be spelled out

2. Of the following items, the one which should NOT be omitted from a typed inter-office memorandum is the
   A. salutation
   B. complementary closing
   C. formal signature
   D. names of those to receive copies

3. A typed rough draft should be double-spaced and should have wide margins PRIMARILY in order to
   A. save time in making typing corrections
   B. provide room for making insertions and corrections
   C. insure that the report is well-organized
   D. permit faster typing of the draft

4. In tabular reports, when a main heading, secondary heading, and single line of columnar headings are used, a triple space (2 blank lines) would be used after the _____ heading(s).
   A. main
   B. secondary
   C. columnar
   D. main and secondary

5. You have been requested to type a letter to Mr. Brown, a district attorney of a small town.
   Of the following, the CORRECT salutation to use is Dear
   A. District Attorney Brown:
   B. Mr. District Attorney:
   C. Mr. Brown:
   D. Honorable Brown:

6. A form letter that is sent to the public can be made to look more personal in appearance by doing all of the following EXCEPT
   A. using a meter stamp on the envelope of the letter
   B. having the letter signed with pen and ink
   C. using a good quality of paper for the letter
   D. matching the type used in the letter with that used for fill-ins

7. A senior typist opens a word-processing application to instruct a typist to create   7.____
a table that contains three column headings. Under each column heading are
three items.
Of the following, which sequence should the senior typist tell the typist to use
when creating this table?
   A. First type the headings, and then type the items under them, a column at
      a time
   B. type each heading with its column of items under it, one column at a time
   C. first type the column of items, then center the headings above them
   D. type the headings and items across the page line by line

8. When a letter is addressed to an agency and a particular person should see it,   8.____
an *attention line* is used.
This attention line is USUALLY found
   A. on the envelope only
   B. above the address
   C. below the address
   D. after the agency named in the address

9. The typing technique of *justifying* is used to   9.____
   A. decide how wide margins of different sized letters should be
   B. make all the lines of copy end evenly on the right-hand margin
   C. center headings above columns on tabular typed material
   D. condense the amount of space that is needed to make a manuscript look
      presentable

10. The date line on a letter is typed correctly when the date is ALL on one line   10.____
   A. with the month written out   B. with slashes between the numbers
   C. and the month is abbreviated   D. with a period at the end

11. When considering how wide to make a column when typing a table, the   11.____
BASIC rule to follow is that the column should be as wide as the longest
   A. item in the body of the column
   B. heading of all of the columns
   C. item in the body or heading of that column
   D. heading or the longest item in the body of any column on that page

12. When a lengthy quotation is included in a letter or a report, it must be   12.____
indicated that it is quoted material. This may be done by
   A. enclosing the quotation in parentheses
   B. placing an exclamation point at the end of the quotation
   C. using the apostrophe marks
   D. indenting from the regular margins on the left and right

13. In order to reach the highest rate of speed and the greatest degree of accuracy while typing, it is LEAST important to
    A. maintain good posture
    B. keep the hands and arms at a comfortable level
    C. strike the keys evenly
    D. keep the typing action in the wrists

13.____

14. It has been shown that the rate of typing and dictation drops when the secretary is not familiar with the language or topic of the copy.
    A practice that a supervisor might BEST advise to improve the knowledge and therefore increase the rate of typing dictation for such material would be for the secretary to
    A. plan a conference with her supervisor to discuss the subject matter
    B. read and review correspondence and related technical journals that come into the office
    C. recopy or retype previously transcribed material as practice
    D. withdraw sample materials from the files to take home for study

14.____

15. The one of the following in which the tab key is NOT generally used is the
    A. placement of the complimentary close and signature line
    B. indentation of paragraphs
    C. placement of the date line
    D. centering of title headings

15.____

16. In order for a business letter to be effective, it is LEAST important that it
    A. say what is meant simply and directly
    B. be written in formal language
    C. include all information the receiver needs to know
    D. be courteously written

16.____

17. If you are momentarily called away from your desk while typing a report of a confidential nature, you should cover or turn the copy over and
    A. remove the page being typed from the computer and file the report
    B. ask someone to watch your desk for you
    C. close the document so that the page is not visible
    D. spread a folder over the computer screen to conceal it

17.____

18. When typing a table that contains a column of figures and a column of words, the PROPER alignment of the column of figures and the column of words should be an even _____ the column of words.
    A. right-hand edge for the column of numbers and an even left-hand edge for
    B. right-hand edge for both the column of numbers and
    C. left-hand edge for the column of numbers and an even right-hand edge for
    D. left-hand edge for both the column of numbers and

18.____

19. The word *re*, when used in a memorandum, refers to the information that is on the _____ line.
    A. identification   B. subject   C. attention   D. reference

19._____

20. Of the following uses of the period, the one which requires NO spacing after it when it is typed is when the period
    A. follows an abbreviation or an initial
    B. follows a figure or letter at the beginning of a line in a list of items
    C. comes between the initials that make up a single abbreviation
    D. comes at the end of a sentence

20._____

21. This mark is a proofreader's mark meaning the word
    A. is misspelled
    B. should be underlined
    C. should be bold
    D. should be capitalized

21._____

22. When typing a report that is double-spaced, the STANDARD recommended practice for indicating the start of new paragraphs is to
    A. double-space between paragraphs and indent the first word at least five spaces
    B. triple-space between paragraphs and indent the first word at least five spaces
    C. triple-space between paragraphs and type block style at the margin
    D. double-space between paragraphs and type block style at the margin

22._____

23. In order to center a heading on a sheet of paper once the center of the paper has been found, the EASIEST and MOST efficient method to use is
    A. note the scale at each end of the heading to be centered and divide by two
    B. backspace from the center of the paper one space for every two letters and spaces in the heading
    C. arrange the heading around the middle number on the computer
    D. use a ruler to mark off the amount of space from both sides of the center of the paper that should be taken up by the heading

23._____

24. You are about to type a single-spaced letter from a typewritten draft.
    In order to center this letter from top to bottom, your FIRST step should be to
    A. determine the number of spaces needed for the top and bottom margins
    B. determine the number of spaces needed for the left and right margins
    C. count the number of lines, including blank ones, which will be used for the letter
    D. subtract from the number of writing lines on the sheet of paper the number of lines that will not be used for the letter

24._____

25. When typing a table which lists several amounts of money and the total in a column, the dollar sign should be placed in front of the
    A. first dollar amount only
    B. total dollar amount only
    C. first and total dollar amounts only
    D. all of the amounts of money in the column

25._____

26. If a legal document is being prepared and requires necessary information to be typed into blank areas on preprinted legal forms, the margins for a line of typewritten material should be determined PRIMARILY by
    A. counting the total number of words to be typed
    B. the margins set for the pre-printed matter
    C. spacing backwards from the right margin rule
    D. the estimated width and height of the material to be entered

26.____

27. When checking for errors in material you've typed, it is BEST to
    A. proofread the material and use the spell-check function in combination
    B. give the material to someone else to review
    C. run the spell-check function and auto-correct all found errors
    D. proofread the material then e-mail it to another typist for final approval

27.____

28. Assume that Mr. Frank Foran is an acting official. In a letter written to him, the word *acting* would
    A. be used with the title in the address and in the salutation
    B. not be used with the title in the address
    C. be used with the title in the address but not in the salutation
    D. not be used with the title in the address or in the salutation

28.____

29. The software program that requires proficiency in typing in order to best utilize its MOST important features is
    A. Microsoft Excel   B. Adobe Reader
    C. Microsoft Word   D. Intuit QuickBooks

29.____

30. The MAIN reason for keeping a careful record of incoming mail is that
    A. greater speed and accuracy is obtained for answering outgoing mail
    B. this record is legal evidence
    C. it develops the efficiency of the office clerks
    D. the information may be useful some day

30.____

KEY (CORRECT ANSWERS)

1.	C	11.	C	21.	D
2.	D	12.	D	22.	A
3.	B	13.	D	23.	B
4.	B	14.	B	24.	C
5.	C	15.	D	25.	C
6.	A	16.	B	26.	B
7.	D	17.	C	27.	A
8.	C	18.	A	28.	C
9.	B	19.	B	29.	C
10.	A	20.	C	30.	A

TEST 2

DIRECTIONS: Each question or incomplete statement is followed by several suggested answers or completions. Select the one that BEST answers the question or completes the statement. *PRINT THE LETTER OF THE CORRECT ANSWER IN THE SPACE AT THE RIGHT.*

Questions 1-4.

DIRECTIONS: Questions 1 through 4 are to be answered SOLELY on the basis of the information contained in the following passage which is taken from a typing test.

Modern office methods, geared to ever higher speeds and aimed at ever greater efficiency, are largely the result of the typewriter. The typewriter is a substitute for handwriting; and, in the hands of a skilled typist, not only turns out letters and other documents at least three times faster than a penman can do the work, but turns out the greater volume more uniformly and legibly. With the use of carbon paper and onionskin paper, identical copies can be made at the same time.

The typewriter, besides its effect on the conduct of business and government, has had a very important effect on the position of women. The typewriter has done much to bring women into business and government, and today there are vastly more women than men typists. Many women have used the keys of the typewriter to climb the ladder to responsible managerial positions.

The typewriter, as its name implies, employs type to make an ink impression on paper. For many years, the manual typewriter was the standard machine used. Today, the electric typewriter is dominant, with electronic typewriters, word processors, and computers coming into wider use.

The mechanism of the office manual typewriter includes a set of keys arranged systematically in rows; a semicircular frame of type, connected to the keys by levers; the carriage or paper carrier; a rubber roller called a platen, against which the type strikes; and an inked ribbon which makes the impression of the type character when the key strikes it. This machine, once omnipresent, is an antique today.

1. The above passage mentions a number of good features of the combination of a skilled typist and a typewriter.
   Of the following, the feature which is NOT mentioned in the passage is
   A. speed   B. uniformity   C. reliability   D. legibility

   1._____

2. According to the above passage, a skilled typist can
   A. turn out at least five carbon copies of typed matter
   B. type at least three times faster than a penman can write
   C. type more than 80 words a minute
   D. readily move into a managerial position

   2._____

17

2 (#2)

3. According to the above passage, which of the following is NOT part of the mechanism of a manual typewriter? 3.____
   A. Carbon paper
   B. Paper carrier
   C. Platen
   D. Inked ribbon

4. According to the above passage, the typewriter has helped 4.____
   A. men more than women in business
   B. women in career advancement into management
   C. men and women equally, but women have taken better advantage of it
   D. more women than men, because men generally dislike routine typing work

5. Standard rules for typing spacing have developed through usage. According to these rules, two spaces are left after a(n) 5.____
   A. colon
   B. comma
   C. hyphen
   D. opening parenthesis

6. Assume that you have to type the heading CENTERING TYPED HEADINGS on a piece of paper which extends from 0 to 100 on the typewriter scale. You want the heading to be perfectly centered on the paper.
   In order to find the proper point on the typewriter scale at which to begin typing, you should determine the paper's center point on the typewriter scale and then _____ the number of letters and spaces in the heading. 6.____
   A. add
   B. add one-half
   C. subtract
   D. subtract one-half

7. While typing from a rough draft, the practice of reading a line ahead of what you are now typing is considered to be a 7.____
   A. *good* practice; it may prepare your fingers for the words which you will be typing
   B. *good* practice; it may help you to review the subject matter contained in the material
   C. *poor* practice; it may increase your typing speed so that your accuracy is decreased
   D. *poor* practice; it may cause you to lose your concentration and make errors in the words you are presently typing

8. Assume that you are transcribing a letter and you are not sure how to divide a word at the end of a line you are typing.
   The BEST way to determine where to divide the word is by 8.____
   A. asking your supervisor
   B. asking the person who dictated the letter
   C. checking with other stenographers
   D. looking up the word in a dictionary

9. When taking proper care of a typewriter, it is NOT a desirable action to
   A. clean the feed rolls with a cloth
   B. dust the exterior surface of the machine
   C. oil the rubber parts of the machine
   D. use a type-cleaning brush to clean the keys

10. Of the following, the LEAST desirable action to take when typing a rough draft of a report is to
    A. cross out typing errors instead of erasing them
    B. double or triple space between lines
    C. provide large margins on all sides of the typing paper
    D. use letterhead or onionskin paper

11. The date line of every business letter should indicate the month, the day of the month, and the year.
    The MOST common practice when typing a date line is to type it as
    A. Jan. 12, 2018   B. January 12, 2018
    C. 1-12-18   D. 1/12/18

Questions 12-16.

DIRECTIONS: Questions 12 through 16 are to be answered SOLELY on the basis of the information provided in the following passage.

A written report is a communication of information from one person to another. It is an account of some matter especially investigated, however routine that matter may be. The ultimate basis of any good written report is facts, which became known through observation and verification. Good written reports may seem to be no more than general ideas and opinions. However, in such cases, the facts leading to these opinions were gathered, verified, and reported earlier, and the opinions are dependent upon these facts. Good style, proper form, and emphasis cannot make a good written report out of unreliable information and bad judgments but on the other hand, solid investigation and brilliant thinking are not likely to become very useful until they are effectively communicated to others. If a person's work calls for written reports, then his work is often no better than his written reports.

12. Based on the information in the above passage, it can be concluded that opinions expressed in a report should be
    A. based on facts which are gathered and reported
    B. emphasized repeatedly when they result from a special investigation
    C. kept to a minimum
    D. separated from the body of the report

13. In the above passage, the one of the following which is mentioned as a way of establishing facts is
    A. authority   B. communication
    C. reporting   D. verification

14. According to the above passage, the characteristic shared by ALL written reports is that they are
    A. accounts of routine matters
    B. transmissions of information
    C. reliable and logical
    D. written in proper form

15. Which of the following conclusions can LOGICALLY be drawn from the information given in the above passage?
    A. Brilliant thinking can make up for unreliable information in a report.
    B. One method of judging an individual's work is the quality of the written reports he is required to submit.
    C. Proper form and emphasis can make a good report out of unreliable information.
    D. Good written reports that seem to be no more than general ideas should be rewritten.

16. Which of the following suggested titles would be MOST appropriate for this passage?
    A. GATHERING AND ORGANIZING FACTS
    B. TECHNIQUES OF OBSERVATION
    C. NATURE AND PURPOSE OF REPORTS
    D. REPORTS AND OPINIONS: DIFFERENCES AND SIMILARITIES

Questions 17-25

DIRECTIONS: Each of Questions 17 through 25 consists of a sentence which may or may not be an example of good English usage. Examine each sentence, considering grammar, punctuation, spelling, capitalization, and awkwardness. Then choose the correct statement about it from the four choices below it. If the English usage in the sentence given is better than any of the changes suggested in Choices B, C, or D, pick choice A. Do NOT pick a choice that will change the meaning of the sentence.

17. We attended a staff conference on Wednesday the new safety and fire rules were discussed.
    A. This is an example of acceptable writing.
    B. The words *safety*, *fire*, and *rules* should begin with capital letters.
    C. There should be a comma after the word *Wednesday*.
    D. There should be a period after the word *Wednesday*, and the word *the* should begin with a capital letter.

18. Neither the dictionary or the telephone directory could be found in the office library.
    A. This is an example of acceptable writing.
    B. The word *or* should be changed to *nor*.
    C. The word *library* should be spelled *libery*.
    D. The word *neither* should be changed to *either*.

19. The report would have been typed correctly if the typist cold read the draft. 19.____
    A. This is an example of acceptable writing.
    B. The word *would* should be removed.
    C. The word *have* should be inserted after the word *could*.
    D. The word *correctly* should be changed to *correct*.

20. The supervisor brought the reports and forms to an employees desk. 20.____
    A. This is an example of acceptable writing.
    B. The word *brought* should be changed to *took*.
    C. There should be a comma after the word *reports* and a comma after the word *forms*.
    D. The word *employees* should be spelled *employee's*.

21. It's important for all the office personnel to submit their vacation schedules on time. 21.____
    A. This is an example of acceptable writing.
    B. The word *It's* should be spelled *Its*.
    C. The word *their* should be spelled *they're*.
    D. The word *personnel* should be spelled *personal*.

22. The supervisor wants that all staff members report to the office at 9:00 A.M. 22.____
    A. This is an example of acceptable writing.
    B. The word *that* should be removed and the word *to* should be inserted after the word *members*.
    C. There should be a comma after the word *wants* and a comma after the word *office*.
    D. The word *wants* should be changed to *want* and the word *shall* should be inserted after the word *members*.

23. Every morning the clerk opens the office mail and distributes it. 23.____
    A. This is an example of acceptable writing.
    B. The word *opens* should be changed to *open*.
    C. The word *mail* should be changed to *letters*.
    D. The word *it* should be changed to *them*.

24. The secretary typed more fast on an electric typewriter than on a manual typewriter. 24.____
    A. This is an example of acceptable writing.
    B. The words *more fast* should be changed to *faster*.
    C. There should be a comma after the words *electric typewriter*.
    D. The word *than* should be changed to *then*.

25. The new stenographer needed a desk a typewriter, a chair and a blotter. 25.____
    A. This is an example of acceptable writing.
    B. The word *blotter* should be spelled *blodder*.
    C. The word *stenographer* should begin with a capital letter.
    D. There should be a comma after the word *desk*.

KEY (CORRECT ANSWERS)

1.	C	11.	B
2.	B	12	A
3.	A	13.	D
4.	B	14.	B
5.	A	15.	B
6.	D	16.	C
7.	D	17.	D
8.	D	18.	B
9.	C	19.	C
10.	D	20.	D

21. A
22. B
23. A
24. B
25. D

EXAMINATION SECTION
TEST 1

DIRECTIONS: Each question or incomplete statement is followed by several suggested answers or completions. Select the one that BEST answers the question or completes the statement. *PRINT THE LETTER OF THE CORRECT ANSWER IN THE SPACE AT THE RIGHT.*

Questions 1-10.

WORD MEANING

DIRECTIONS: Each question from 1 to 10 contains a word in capitals followed by four suggested meanings of the word. For each question, choose the best meaning. *PRINT THE LETTER OF THE CORRECT ANSWER IN THE SPACE AT THE RIGHT.*

1. ACCURATE
    A. correct　　B. useful　　C. afraid　　D. careless

2. ALTER
    A. copy　　B. change　　C. report　　D. agree

3. DOCUMENT
    A. outline　　B. agreement　　C. blueprint　　D. record

4. INDICATE
    A. listen　　B. show　　C. guess　　D. try

5. INVENTORY
    A. custom　　B. discovery　　C. warning　　D. list

6. ISSUE
    A. annoy　　B. use up　　C. give out　　D. gain

7. NOTIFY
    A. inform　　B. promise　　C. approve　　D. strengthen

8. ROUTINE
    A. path　　B. mistake　　C. habit　　D. journey

9. TERMINATE
    A. rest　　B. start　　C. deny　　D. end

10. TRANSMIT
    A. put in　　B. send　　C. stop　　D. go across

Questions 11-15.

READING COMPREHENSION

DIRECTIONS: Questions 11 through 15 test how well you understand what you read. It will be necessary for you to read carefully because your answers to these questions should be based ONLY on the information given in the following paragraphs.

The recipient gains an impression of a typewritten letter before he begins to read the message. Pastors which provide for a good first impression include margins and spacing that are visually pleasing, formal parts of the letter which are correctly placed according to the style of the letter, copy which is free of obvious erasures and over-strikes, and transcript that is even and clear. The problem for the typist is that of how to produce that first, positive impression of her work.

There are several general rules which a typist can follow when she wishes to prepare a properly spaced letter on a sheet of letter-head. Ordinarily, the width of a letter should not be less than four inches nor more than six inches. The side margins should also have a desirable relation to the bottom margin and the space between the letterhead and the body of the letter. Usually the most appealing arrangement is when the side margins are even and the bottom margin is slightly wider than the side margins. In some offices, however, standard line length is used for all business letters, and the secretary then varies the spacing between the date line and the inside address according to the length of the letter.

11. The BEST title for the above paragraphs would be:
    A. Writing Office Letters
    B. Making Good First Impressions
    C. Judging Well-Typed Letters
    D. Good Placing and Spacing for Office Letters

12. According to the above paragraphs, which of the following might be considered the way in which people very quickly judge the quality of work which has been typed? By
    A. measuring the margins to see if they are correct
    B. looking at the spacing and cleanliness of the typescript
    C. scanning the body of the letter for meaning
    D. reading the date line and address for errors

13. What, according to the above paragraphs, would be definitely UNDESIRABLE as the average line length of a typed letter?
    A. 4"   B. 5"   C. 6"   D. 7"

14. According to the above paragraphs, when the line length is kept standard, the secretary
    A. does not have to vary the spacing at all since this also is standard
    B. adjusts the spacing between the date line and inside address for different lengths of letters
    C. uses the longest line as a guideline for spacing between the date line and inside address
    D. varies the number of spaces between the lines

3 (#1)

15. According to the above paragraphs, side margins are MOST pleasing when they
    A. are even and somewhat smaller than the bottom margin
    B. are slightly wider than the bottom margin
    C. vary with the length of the letter
    D. are figured independently from the letterhead and the body of the letter

Questions 16-20.

CODING

DIRECTIONS:

Name of Applicant	H A N G S B R U K E
Test Code	c o m p l e x i t y
File Number	0 1 2 3 4 5 6 7 8 9

Assume that each of the above capital letters is the first letter of the name of an Applicant, that the small letter directly beneath each capital letter is the test code for the Applicant, and that the number directly beneath each code letter is the file number for the Applicant.

In each of the following Questions 16 through 20, the test code letters and the file numbers in Columns 2 and 3 should correspond to the capital letters in Column 1. For each question, look at each column carefully and mark your answer as follows:

If there is an error only in Column 2, mark your answer A.
If there is an error only in Column 3, mark your answer B.
If there is an error in both Columns 2 and 3, mark your answer C.
If both Columns 2 and 3 are correct, mark your answer D.

The following sample question is given to help you understand the procedure.

SAMPLE QUESTION

Column 1	Column 2	Column 3
AKEHN	otyci	18902

In Column 2, the final test code letter *i.* should be m. Column 3 is correctly coded to Column 1. Since there is an error only in Column 2, the answer is A.

	Column 1	Column 2	Column 3
16.	NEKKU	mytti	29987
17.	KRAEB	txyle	86095
18.	ENAUK	ymoit	92178
19.	REANA	xeomo	69121
20.	EKHSE	ytcxy	97049

4 (#1)

Questions 21-30.

ARITHMETICAL REASONING

21. If a secretary answered 28 phone calls and typed the addresses for 112 credit statements in one morning, what is the ratio of phone calls answered to credit statements typed for that period of time?

    A. 1:4   B. 1:7   C. 2:3   D. 3:5

22. According to a suggested filing system, no more than 10 folders should be filed behind any one file guide and from 15 to 25 file guides should be used in each file drawer for easy finding and filing.
    The maximum number of folders that a five-drawer file cabinet can hold to allow easy finding and filing is

    A. 550   B. 750   C. 1,100   D. 1,250

23. An employee had a starting salary of $25,804. He received a salary increase at the end of each year, and at the end of the seventh year his salary was $33,476.
    What was his average annual increase in salary over these seven years?

    A. $1,020   B. $1,076   C. $1,096   D. $1,144

24. The 55 typists and 28 senior clerks in a certain city agency were paid a total of $1,943,200 in salaries last year.
    If the average annual salary of a typist was $22,400 the average annual salary of a senior clerk was

    A. $25,400   B. $26,600   C. $26,800   D. $27,000

25. A typist has been given a three page report to type. She has finished typing the first two pages. The first page has 283 words, and the second page has 366 words.
    If the total report consists of 954 words, how many words will she have to type on the third page of the report?

    A. 202   B. 287   C. 305   D. 313

26. In one day, Clerk A processed 30% more forms than Clerk 8, and Clerk C processed 1 1/4 times as many forms as Clerk A. If Clerk B processed 40 forms, how many more forms were processed by Clerk C than Clerk B?

    A. 12   B. 13   C. 21   D. 25

27. A clerk who earns a gross salary of $452 every two weeks has the following deductions taken from her paycheck:
    15% for City, State, Federal taxes; 2 1/2% for Social Security; $1.30 for health insurance; and $6.00 for union dues. The amount of her take-home pay is

    A. $256.20   B. $312.40   C. $331.60   D. $365.60

28. In 2020, a city agency spent $2,000 to buy pencils at a cost of $5.00 a dozen.
    If the agency used 3/4 of these pencils in 2020 and used the same number of pencils in 2021, how many more pencils did it have to buy to have enough pencils for all of 2021?

    A. 1,200   B. 2,400   C. 3,600   D. 4,800

29. A clerk who worked in Agency X earned the following salaries: $20,140 the first year, $21,000 the second year, and $21,920 the third year. Another clerk who worked in Agency Y for three years earned $21,100 a year for two years and $21,448 the third year. The difference between the average salaries received by both clerks over a three-year period is

    A. $196 B. $204 C. $348 D. $564

30. An employee who works over 40 hours in any week receives overtime payment for the extra hours at time and one-half (1 1/2 times) his hourly rate of pay. An employee who earns $13.60 an hour works a total of 45 hours during a certain week.
    His total pay for that week would be

    A. $564.40 B. $612.00 C. $646.00 D. $812.00

Questions 31-35.

RELATED INFORMATION

31. To tell a newly-employed clerk to fill a top drawer of a four-drawer cabinet with heavy folders which will be often used and to keep lower drawers only partly filled is

    A. *good,* because a tall person would have to bend unnecessarily if he had to use a lower drawer
    B. *bad,* because the file cabinet may tip over when the top drawer is opened
    C. *good,* because it is the most easily reachable drawer for the average person
    D. *bad,* because a person bending down at another drawer may accidentally bang his head on the bottom of the drawer when he straightens up

32. If a senior typist or senior clerk has requisitioned a *ream* of paper in order to duplicate a single page office announcement, how many announcements can be printed from the one package of paper?

    A. 200 B. 500 C. 700 0. 1,000

33. Your supervisor has asked you to locate a telephone number for an attorney named Jones, whose office is located at 311 Broadway, and whose name is not already listed in your files.
    The BEST method for finding the number would be for you to

    A. call the information operator and have her get it for you
    B. look in the alphabetical directory (white pages) under the name Jones at 311 Broadway
    C. refer to the heading Attorney in the yellow pages for the name Jones at 311 Broadway
    D. ask your supervisor who referred her to Mr. Jones, then call that person for the number

34. An example of material that should NOT be sent by first class mail is a

    A. email copy of a letter   B. post card
    C. business reply card   D. large catalogue

35. In the operations of a government agency, a voucher is ORDINARILY used to

    A. refer someone to the agency for a position or assignment
    B. certify that an agency's records of financial trans-actions are accurate
    C. order payment from agency funds of a stated amount to an individual
    D. enter a statement of official opinion in the records of the agency

Questions 36-40.

ENGLISH USAGE

DIRECTIONS: Each question from 36 through 40 contains a sentence. Read each sentence carefully to decide whether it is correct. Then, in the space at the right, mark your answer:

(A) if the sentence is incorrect because of bad grammar or sentence structure

(B) if the sentence is incorrect because of bad punctuation

(C) if the sentence is incorrect because of bad capitalization

(D) if the sentence is correct

Each incorrect sentence has only one type of error. Consider a sentence correct if it has no errors, although there may be other correct ways of saying the same thing.

SAMPLE QUESTION I: One of our clerks were promoted yesterday.

The subject of this sentence is one, so the verb should be *was promoted* instead of *were promoted*. Since the sentence is incorrect because of bad grammar, the answer to Sample Question I is (A).

SAMPLE QUESTION II: Between you and me, I would prefer not going there.

Since this sentence is correct, the answer to Sample Question II is (D).

36. The National alliance of Businessmen is trying to persuade private businesses to hire youth in the summertime.

37. The supervisor who is on vacation, is in charge of processing vouchers.

38. The activity of the committee at its conferences is always stimulating.

39. After checking the addresses again, the letters went to the mailroom.

40. The director, as well as the employees, are interested in sharing the dividends.

Questions 41-45.

FILING

DIRECTIONS: Each question from 41 through 45 contains four names. For each question, choose the name that should be FIRST if the four names are to be arranged in alphabetical order in accordance with the Rules for Alphabetical Filing given below. Read these rules carefully. Then, for each question, indicate in the space at the right the letter before the name that should be FIRST in alphabetical order.

RULES FOR ALPHABETICAL FILING

Names of People

(1) The names of people are filed in strict alphabetical order, first according to the last name, then according to first name or initial, and finally according to middle name or initial. FOR EXAMPLE: George Allen comes before Edward Bell, and Leonard P. Reston comes before Lucille B. Reston.

(2) When last names are the same, FOR EXAMPLE, A. Green and Agnes Green, the one with the initial comes before the one with the name written out when the first initials are identical.

(3) When first and last names are alike and the middle name is given, FOR EXAMPLE, John David Doe and John Devoe Doe, the names should be filed in the alphabetical order of the middle names.

(4) When first and last names are the same, a name without a middle initial comes before one with a middle name or initial. FOR EXAMPLE, John Doe comes before both John A. Doe and John Alan Doe.

(5) When first and last names are the same, a name with a middle initial comes before one with a middle name beginning with the same initial. FOR EXAMPLE: Jack R. Hertz comes before Jack Richard Hertz.

(6) Prefixes such as De, O', Mac, Mc, and Van are filed as written and are treated as part of the names to which they are connected. FOR EXAMPLE: Robert O'Dea is filed before David Olsen.

(7) Abbreviated names are treated as if they were spelled out. FOR EXAMPLE: Chas. is filed as Charles and Thos. is filed as Thomas.

(8) Titles and designations such as Dr., Mr., and Prof. are disregarded in filing.

Names of Organizations

(1) The names of business organizations are filed according to the order in which each word in the name appears. When an organization name bears the name of a person, it is filed according to the rules for filing names of people as given above. FOR EXAMPLE: William Smith Service Co. comes before Television Distributors, Inc.

(2) Where bureau, board, office, or department appears as the first part of the title of a governmental agency, that agency should be filed under the word in the title expressing the chief function of the agency FOR EXAMPLE: Bureau of the Budget would be filed as if written Budget, (Bureau of the). The Department of Personnel would be filed as if written Personnel, (Department of).

(3) When the following words are part of an organization, they are disregarded: the, of, and.

(4) When there are numbers in a name, they are treated as if they were spelled out. FOR EXAMPLE: 10th Street Bootery is filed as Tenth Street Bootery.

SAMPLE QUESTION:
    A. Jane Earl (2)
    B. James A. Earle (4)
    C. James Earl (1)
    D. J. Earle (3)

The numbers in parentheses show the proper alphabetical order in which these names should be filed. Since the name that should be filed FIRST is James Earl, the answer to the Sample Question is (C).

41.
    A. Majorca Leather Goods
    B. Robert Maiorca and Sons
    C. Maintenance Management Corp.
    D. Majestic Carpet Mills

42.
    A. Municipal Telephone Service
    B. Municipal Reference Library
    C. Municipal Credit Union
    D. Municipal Broadcasting System

43.
    A. Robert B. Pierce   B. R. Bruce Pierce
    C. Ronald Pierce   D. Robert Bruce Pierce

44.
    A. Four Seasons Sports Club   B. 14th. St. Shopping Center
    C. Forty Thieves Restaurant   D. 42nd St. Theaters

45.
    A. Franco Franceschini   B. Amos Franchini
    C. Sandra Franceschia   D. Lilie Franchinesca

Questions 46-50.

SPELLING

DIRECTIONS: In each question, one of the words is misspelled. Select the letter of the misspelled word. *PRINT THE LETTER OF THE CORRECT ANSWER IN THE SPACE AT THE RIGHT.*

46.
    A. option   B. extradite
    C. comparitive   D. jealousy

47.
    A. handicaped   B. assurance
    C. sympathy   D. speech

48. A. recommend
    C. disapprove
    B. carraige
    D. independent

49. A. ingenuity
    C. uncanny
    B. tenet (opinion)
    D. intrigueing

50. A. arduous
    C. iervant
    B. hideous
    D. companies

KEY (CORRECT ANSWERS)

1. A	11. D	21. A	31. B	41. C
2. B	12. B	22. D	32. B	42. D
3. D	13. D	23. C	33. C	43. B
4. B	14. B	24. A	34. D	44. D
5. D	15. A	25. C	35. C	45. C
6. C	16. B	26. D	36. C	46. C
7. A	17. C	27. D	37. B	47. A
8. C	18. D	28. B	38. D	48. B
9. D	19. A	29. A	39. A	49. D
10. B	20. C	30. C	40. A	50. C

EXAMINATION SECTION

DIRECTIONS: Each question or incomplete statement is followed by several suggested answers or completions. Select the one that BEST answers the question or completes the statement. *PRINT THE LETTER OF THE CORRECT ANSWER IN THE SPACE AT THE RIGHT.*

Questions 1-15:
For each of the following questions, PRINT on the space at the right the word TRUE if the statement is true, or FALSE if the statement is false.

1. A typist who discovers an obvious grammatical error in a report she is typing should, under ordinary circumstances, copy the material as it was given to her.   1._____

2. The initials of the typist who typed a business letter generally appear on the letter.   2._____

3. It is considered POOR letter form to have *only* the complimentary close and the signature on the second page of a business letter.   3._____

4. Correspondence which is filed according to dates of letters is said to be filed chronologically.   4._____

5. It is *usually* unnecessary to proofread punctuation marks in a report.   5._____

6. The use of window envelopes *reduces* probability of mailing a letter to the wrong address.   6._____

7. Letter size paper is *usually* longer than legal size paper.   7._____

8. It is considered GOOD typing form to have two spaces following a comma.   8._____

9. Both sheets of a two-page typed letter MUST be letterheads.   9._____

10. Before removing a typed letter from the typewriter, the typist should read the copy so that corrections may be made neatly.   10._____

11. When alphabetizing names, you should ALWAYS disregard first names.   11._____

12. When filing a large number of cards according to the name on each card, it is generally a *good* procedure to alphabetize the cards FIRST.   12._____

13. When a report may be filed in a subject file under two headings, it is *good* practice to make a cross reference.   13._____

33

14. If an essential point has been omitted in a business letter, it is usually considered *good* letter form to include this point in a brief postscript. 14._____

15. Rough draft copies of a report should generally be single-spaced. 15._____

Questions 16-22:
The following items consist of problems in arithmetic. Print in the space at the right the word TRUE if the statement is true, and FALSE if the statement is false.

16. If the rate for first-class mail is 37 cents for each ounce or fraction of an ounce and 23 cents for each ounce or fraction of an ounce above one ounce, then the total cost of sending by first-class mail three letters weighing 1-1/2 ounces, 2 ounces, and 2-1/2 ounces, respectively, would be $1.80. 16._____

17. A typist, who in one hour typed a report consisting of five pages with 60 lines per page and 10 words per line, would have typed at the rate of 45 words per minute. 17._____

18. If a department store employs 45 clerks, 21 typists, and 18 stenographers, the percentage of these employees who are typists is 25%. 18._____

19. If four typists, who type at the same rate of speed, type 1,000 letters in 12 hours, then it will take six typists nine hours to type 1,000 letters. 19._____

20. If 15% of a stenographer's time is spent in taking dictation and 45% of her time is taken up in transcribing her notes, then she has a remainder of two-fifths of her time for performing other duties. 20._____

21. A typist completed 14 pages of a 24-page report before being asked to speak briefly with her employer, then typed the remaining 10 pages. Up until the time she spoke with her employer, the typist had already completed approximately 58% of the report. 21._____

22. Employee A types at a rate of 48 words per minute, while Employee B types at a rate of 54 words per minute. If both employees spend exactly 2-1/4 hours typing reports, Employee B will have typed approximately 810 more words than Employee A. 22._____

Questions 23-54:
Each of the following items consists of two words preceded by the letters A and B. In each item, *one* of the words may be spelled INCORRECTLY, or *both* words may be spelled CORRECTLY. If one of the words is spelled incorrectly, print in the space at the right the letter corresponding to the incorrect word. If both are spelled correctly, print the answer C.

23. A. accessible	B. artifical	23._____
24. A. feild	B. arranged	24._____
25. A. admittence	B. hastily	25._____
26. A. easely	B. readily	26._____
27. A. pursue	B. decend	27._____
28. A. measure	B. laboratory	28._____
29. A. exausted	B. traffic	29._____
30. A. discussion	B. unpleasant	30._____
31. A. campaign	B. murmer	31._____
32. A. guarantee	B. sanatary	32._____
33. A. communication	B. safty	33._____
34. A. numerus	B. celebration	34._____
35. A. nourish	B. begining	35._____
36. A. courious	B. witness	36._____
37. A. undoubtedly	B. thoroughly	37._____
38. A. justified	B. offering	38._____
39. A. predjudice	B. license	39._____
40. A. label	B. pamphlet	40._____
41. A. bulletin	B. physical	41._____
42. A. assure	B. exceed	42._____
43. A. advantagous	B. evident	43._____

44. A. benefit   B. occured   44. _____

45. A. acquire   B. graditude   45. _____

46. A. amenable   B. boundry   46. _____

47. A. deceive   B. voluntary   47. _____

48. A. imunity   B. conciliate   48. _____

49. A. acknoledge   B. presume   49. _____

50. A. substitute   B. prespiration   50. _____

51. A. reputible   B. announce   51. _____

52. A. luncheon   B. wretched   52. _____

53. A. regrettable   B. proficiency   53. _____

54. A. rescind   B. dissappoint   54. _____

Questions 55-72:
Each of the sentences that follow may be classified MOST appropriately under one of the following three categories:
    A. *faulty* because of incorrect grammar
    B. *faulty* because of incorrect punctuation
    C. *correct*

Examine each sentence, then select the best answer as listed above and place the letter in the space at the right. All incorrect sentences contain only ONE type of error. Consider a sentence correct if it contains none of the types of errors mentioned, even though there may be other correct ways of expressing the same thought.

55. He sent the notice to the clerk who hired you yesterday.   55. _____

56. It must be admitted, however that you were not informed of this change.   56. _____

57. Only the employees who have served in this grade for at least two years are eligible for promotion.   57. _____

58. The work was divided equally between she and Mary.   58. _____

59. He thought that you were not available at the time.   59. _____

60. When the messenger returns; please give him this package.   60. _____

61. The new secretary prepared, typed, addressed, and delivered, the notices.

62. Walking into the room, his desk can be seen at the rear.

63. Although John has worked here longer then she, he produces a smaller amount of work.

64. She said she could of typed this report yesterday.

65. Neither one of these procedures are adequate for the efficient performance of this task.

66. The typewriter is the tool of the typist; the cash register, the tool of the cashier.

67. "The assignment must be completed as soon as possible" said the supervisor.

68. As you know, office handbooks are issued to all new employees.

69. Writing a speech is sometimes easier than to deliver it before an audience.

70. Mr. Brown our accountant, will audit the accounts next week.

71. Give the assignment to whomever is able to do it most efficiently.

72. The supervisor expected either your or I to file these reports.

Questions 73-90:
For each of the following test items, print the letter in the space at the right of the answer that BEST completes the statement.

73. A PREVALENT practice is one which is
    A. rare   B. unfair   C. widespread   D. correct

74. To prepare a RECAPITULATION means *most nearly* to prepare a
    A. summary   B. revision   C. defense   D. decision

75. An ADVERSE decision is one which is
    A. unfavorable   B. unwise
    C. anticipated   D. backwards

76. A COMMENDATORY report is one which
    A. expresses praise   B. contains contradictions
    C. is too detailed   D. is threatening

77. "The council will DEFER action on this matter." The word DEFER means *most nearly*
    A. hasten   B. consider   C. postpone   D. reject

78. MEAGER results are those which are
    A. satisfactory   B. scant
    C. unexpected   D. praiseworthy

79. An ARDUOUS job assignment
    A. requires much supervision   B. is laborious
    C. absorbs one's interest   D. is lengthy

80. "This employee was IMPLICATED." The word IMPLICATED *most nearly* means
    A. demoted   B. condemned   C. involved   D. accused

81. To be DETAINED means *most nearly* to be
    A. entertained   B. held back
    C. sent away   D. scolded

82. An AMIABLE person is one who is
    A. active   B. pleasing   C. thrifty   D. foolish

83. A UNIQUE procedure is one which is
    A. simple   B. uncommon   C. useless   D. ridiculous

84. The word REPLENISH means *most nearly* to
    A. give up   B. punish   C. refill   D. empty

85. A CONCISE report is one which is
    A. logical   B. favorable   C. brief   D. intelligent

86. ELATED means *most nearly*
    A. lengthened   B. matured   C. excited   D. youthful

87. SANCTION means *most nearly*
    A. approval   B. delay   C. priority   D. veto

88. EGOTISTIC means *most nearly*
    A. tiresome   B. self-centered
    C. sly   D. smartly attired

89. TRITE means *most nearly*
    A. brilliant   B. unusual
    C. funny   D. commonplace

90. FESTIVE means *most nearly*
    A. edible   B. joyous   C. proud   D. serene

KEY (CORRECT ANSWERS)

1. F	31. B	61. B
2. T	32. B	62. A
3. T	33. B	63. C
4. T	34. A	64. A
5. F	35. B	65. A
6. T	36. A	66. C
7. F	37. C	67. B
8. F	38. C	68. C
9. F	39. A	69. A
10. T	40. C	70. B
11. F	41. C	71. A
12. T	42. C	72. A
13. T	43. A	73. C
14. F	44. B	74. A
15. F	45. B	75. A
16. F	46. B	76. A
17. F	47. C	77. C
18. T	48. A	78. B
19. F	49. A	79. B
20. T	50. B	80. C
21. T	51. A	81. B
22. T	52. C	82. B
23. B	53. C	83. B
24. A	54. B	84. C
25. A	55. A	85. C
26. A	56. B	86. C
27. B	57. C	87. A
28. C	58. A	88. B
29. A	59. C	89. D
30. C	60. B	90. B

EXAMINATION SECTION
TEST 1

DIRECTIONS: Each question or incomplete statement is followed by several suggested answers or completions. Select the one that BEST answers the question or completes the statement. *PRINT THE LETTER OF THE CORRECT ANSWER IN THE SPACE AT THE RIGHT.*

Questions 1-4.

DIRECTIONS: Questions 1 through 4 are to be answered SOLELY on the basis of the following passage.

    Job analysis combined with performance appraisal is an excellent method of determining training needs of individuals. The steps in this method are to determine the specific duties of the job, to evaluate the adequacy with which the employee performs each of these duties, and finally to determine what significant improvements can be made by training.
    The list of duties can be obtained in a number of ways: asking the employee, asking the supervisor, observing the employee, etc. Adequacy of performance can be estimated by the employee, but the supervisor's evaluation must also be obtained. This evaluation will usually be based on observation.
    What does the supervisor observe? The employee, while he is working; the employee's work relationships; the ease, speed, and sureness of the employee's actions; the way he applies himself to the job; the accuracy and amount of completed work; its conformity with established procedures and standards; the appearance of the work; the soundness of judgment it shows; and, finally, signs of good or poor communication, understanding, and cooperation among employees.
    Such observation is a normal and inseparable part of the everyday job of supervision. Systematically, recorded, evaluated, and summarized, it highlights both general and individual training needs.

1. According to the passage, job analysis may be used by the supervisor in
   A. increasing his own understanding of tasks performed in his unit
   B. increasing efficiency of communication within the organization
   C. assisting personnel experts in the classification of positions
   D. determining in which areas an employee needs more instruction

1.____

2. According to the passage, the FIRST step in determining the training needs of employees is to
   A. locate the significant improvements that can be made by training
   B. determine the specific duties required in a job
   C. evaluate the employee's performance
   D. motivate the employee to want to improve himself

2.____

3. On the basis of the above passage, which of the following is the BEST way for a supervisor to determine the adequacy of employee performance?
   A. Check the accuracy and amount of completed work
   B. Ask the training officer
   C. Observe all aspects of the employee's work
   D. Obtain the employee's own estimate

4. Which of the following is NOT mentioned by the passage as a factor to be taken into consideration in judging the adequacy of employee performance?
   A. Accuracy of completed work
   B. Appearance of completed work
   C. Cooperation among employees
   D. Attitude of the employee toward his supervisor

5. In indexing names of business firms and other organizations, ONE of the rules to be followed is:
   A. The word *and* is considered an indexing unit.
   B. When a firm name includes the full name of a person who is not well-known, the person's first name is considered as the first indexing unit.
   C. Usually the units in a firm name are indexed in the order in which they are written.
   D. When a firm's name is made up of single letters (such as ABC Corp.), the letters taken together are considered more than one indexing unit.

6. Assume that people often come to your office with complaints of errors in your agency's handling of their clients. The employees in your office have the job of listening to these complaints and investigating them. One day, when it is almost closing time, a person comes into your office, apparently very angry, and demands that you take care of his complaint at once.
   Your IMMEDIATE reaction should be to
   A. suggest that he return the following day
   B. find out his name and the nature of his complaint
   C. tell him to write a letter
   D. call over your supervisor

7. Assume that part of your job is to notify people concerning whether their applications for a certain program have been approved or disapproved. However, you do not actually make the decision on approval or disapproval. One day, you answer a telephone call from a woman who states that she has not yet received any word on her application. She goes on to tell you her qualifications for the program. From what she has said, you know that persons with such qualifications are usually approved.
   Of the following, which one is the BEST thing for you to say to her?
   A. "You probably will be accepted, but wait until you receive a letter before trying to join the program."
   B. "Since you seem well qualified, I am sure that your application will be approved."

C. "If you can write us a letter emphasizing your qualifications, it may speed up the process."
D. "You will be notified of the results of your application as soon as a decision has been made."

8. Suppose that one of your duties includes answering specific telephone inquiries. Your superior refers a call to you from an irate person who claims that your agency is inefficient and is wasting taxpayers' money.
Of the following, the BEST way to handle such a call is to
   A. listen briefly and then hang up without answering
   B. note the caller's comments and tell him that you will transmit them to your superiors
   C. connect the caller with the head of your agency
   D. discuss your own opinions with the caller

8.____

9. An employee has been assigned to open her division head's mail and place it on his desk. One day, the employee opens a letter which she then notices is marked *Personal*.
Of the following, the BEST action for her to take is to
   A. write *Personal* on the letter and staple the envelope to the back of the letter
   B. ignore the matter and treat the letter the same way as the others
   C. give it to another division head to hold until her own division head comes into the office
   D. leave the letter in the envelope and write *Sorry opened by mistake* on the envelope and initial it

9.____

Questions 10-14.

DIRECTIONS: Questions 10 through 14 each consist of a quotation which contains one word that is incorrectly used because it is not in keeping with the meaning that the quotation is evidently intended to convey. Of the words underlined in each quotation, determine which word is incorrectly used. Then select from among the words lettered A, B, C, and D the word which, when substituted for the incorrectly used word, would BEST help to convey the meaning of the quotation. (Do not indicate a change for an underlined word unless the underlined word is incorrectly used.)

10. Unless reasonable managerial supervision is <u>exercised</u> over office supplies, it is certain that there will be extravagance, <u>rejected</u> items out of stock, <u>excessive</u> prices paid for certain items, and <u>obsolete</u> material in the stockroom.
    A. overlooked   B. immoderate   C. needed   D. instituted

10.____

11. Since <u>office</u> supplies are in such <u>common</u> use, an attitude of indifference about their handling is not <u>unusual</u>. Their importance is often recognized only when they are <u>utilized</u> or out of stock, for office employees must have proper supplies if maximum productivity is to be <u>attained</u>.
    A. plentiful   B. unavailable   C. reduced   D. expected

11.____

12. Anyone <u>effected</u> by paperwork, <u>interested</u> in or engaged in office work, or desiring to improve <u>informational</u> activities can find materials <u>keyed</u> to his needs.
    A. attentive   B. available   C. affected   D. ambitious

13. Information is <u>homogeneous</u> and must therefore be properly classified so that each type may be <u>employed</u> in ways <u>appropriate</u> to its <u>own peculiar</u> properties.
    A. apparent
    B. heterogeneous
    C. consistent
    D. idiosyncratic

14. <u>Intellectual</u> training may seem a <u>formidable</u> phrase, but it means nothing more than the <u>deliberate</u> cultivation of the ability to think, and there is no <u>dark</u> contrast between the intellectual and the practical.
    A. subjective   B. objective   C. sharp   D. vocational

15. The MOST important reason for having a filing system is to
    A. get papers out of the way
    B. have a record of everything that has happened
    C. retain information to justify your actions
    D. enable rapid retrieval of information

16. The system of filing which is used MOST frequently is called _____ filing.
    A. alphabetic
    B. alphanumeric
    C. geographic
    D. numeric

17. One of the clerks under your supervision has been telephoning frequently to tell you that he was taking the day off. Unless there is a real need for it, taking leave which is not scheduled is frowned upon because it upsets the work schedule.
    Under these circumstances, which of the following reasons for taking the day off is MOST acceptable?
    A. "I can't work when my arthritis bothers me."
    B. "I've been pressured with work from my night job and needed the extra time to catch up."
    C. "My family just moved to a new house, and I needed the time to start the repairs."
    D. "Work here has not been challenging, and I've been looking for another job."

18. One of the employees under your supervision, previously a very satisfactory worker, has begun arriving late one or two mornings each week. No explanation has been offered for this change. You call her to your office for a conference. As you are explaining the purpose of the conference and your need to understand this sudden lateness problem, she becomes very angry and states that you have no right to question her.
    Of the following, the BEST course of action for you to take at this point is to

A. inform her in your most authoritarian tone that you are the supervisor and that you have every right to question her
B. end the conference and advise the employee that you will have no further discussion with her until she controls her temper
C. remain calm, try to calm her down, and when she has quieted, explain the reasons for your questions and the need for answers
D. hold your temper; when she has calmed down, tell her that you will not have a tardy worker in your unit and will have her transferred at once

19. Assume that, in the branch of the agency for which you work, you are the only clerical person on the staff with a supervisory title and, in addition, that you are the office manager. On a particular day when all members of the professional staff are away from the building attending an important meeting, an urgent call comes through requesting some confidential information ordinarily released only by professional staff.
    Of the following, the MOST reasonable action for you to take is to
    A. decline to give the information because you are not a member of the professional staff
    B. offer to call back after you get permission from the agency director at the main office
    C. advise the caller that you will supply the information as soon as your chief returns
    D. supply the information requested and inform your chief when she returns

19.____

20. As a supervisor, you are scheduled to attend an important conference with your superior. However, that day you learn that your very capable assistant is ill and unable to come to work. Several highly sensitive tasks are scheduled for completion on this day.
    Of the following, the BEST way to handle this situation is to
    A. tell your supervisor you cannot attend the meeting and ask that it be postponed
    B. assign one of your staff to see that the jobs are completed and turned in
    C. advise your supervisor of the situation and ask what you should do
    D. call the departments for which the work is being done and ask for an extension of time

20.____

21. When a decision needs to be made which is likely to affect units other than his own, a supervisor should USUALLY
    A. make such a decision quickly and then discuss it with his supervisor
    B. make such a decision only after careful consultation with his subordinates
    C. discuss the problem with his immediate superior before making such a decision
    D. have his subordinates arrive at such a decision in conference with the subordinates in the other units

21.____

22. Assume that, as a supervisor in Division X, you are training Ms. Y, a new employee, to answer the telephone properly.
    You should explain that the BEST way to answer is to pick up the receiver and say:

22.____

A. "What is your name, please?" B. "May I help you?"
C. "Ms. Y speaking." D. "Division X, Ms. Y speaking."

Questions 23-25.

DIRECTIONS: Questions 23 through 25 consist of sentences in which two words are missing. Examine each sentence, and then choose from below it the words which should be inserted in the blank spaces in order to create a coherent and well-written sentence.

23. Human behavior is far _____ variable, and therefore _____ predictable, than that of any other species. 23._____
    A. less; as   B. less; not   C. more; not   D. more; less

24. The _____ limitation of this method is that the results are based _____ a narrow sample. 24._____
    A. chief; with   B. chief; on   C. only; for   D. only; to

25. Although there _____ a standard procedure for handling these problems, each case often has _____ own unique features. 25._____
    A. are; its   B. are; their   C. is; its   D. is; their

KEY (CORRECT ANSWERS)

1.	D	11.	B
2.	B	12.	C
3.	C	13.	B
4.	D	14.	C
5.	C	15.	D
6.	B	16.	A
7.	D	17.	A
8.	B	18.	C
9.	D	19.	B
10.	C	20.	C

21. C
22. D
23. D
24. B
25. C

TEST 2

DIRECTIONS: Each question or incomplete statement is followed by several suggested answers or completions. Select the one that BEST answers the question or completes the statement. *PRINT THE LETTER OF THE CORRECT ANSWER IN THE SPACE AT THE RIGHT.*

Questions 1-3.

DIRECTIONS: Questions 1 through 3 each consist of a group of four sentences. Read each sentence carefully, and select the one of the four in each group which represents the BEST English usage for business letters and reports.

1. A. The chairman himself, rather than his aides, has reviewed the report.
    B. The chairman himself, rather than his aides, have reviewed the report.
    C. The chairmen, not the aide, has reviewed the report.
    D. The aide, not the chairmen, have reviewed the report.

2. A. Various proposals were submitted but the decision is not been made.
    B. Various proposals has been submitted but the decision has not been made.
    C. Various proposals were submitted but the decision is not been made.
    D. Various proposals have been submitted but the decision has not been made.

3. A. Everyone were rewarded for his successful attempt.
    B. They were successful in their attempts and each of them was rewarded.
    C. Each of them are rewarded for their successful attempts.
    D. The reward for their successful attempts were made to each of them.

4. Which of the following is MOST suited to arrangement in chronological order?
    A. Applications for various types and levels of jobs
    B. Issues of a weekly publication
    C. Weekly time cards for all employees for the week of April 21
    D. Personnel records for all employees

5. Words that are *synonymous* with a given word ALWAYS _____ the given word.
    A. have the same meaning as   B. have the same pronunciation as
    C. have the opposite meaning of D. can be rhymed with

Questions 6-11.

DIRECTIONS: Questions 6 through 11 are to be answered on the basis of the following chart showing numbers of errors made by four clerks in one work unit for a half-year period.

2 (#2)

	Allan	Barry	Cary	David
July	5	4	1	7
August	8	3	9	8
September	7	8	7	5
October	3	6	5	3
November	2	4	4	6
December	5	2	8	4

6. The clerk with the HIGHEST number of errors for the six-month period was
   A. Allan   B. Barry   C. Cary   D. David

7. If the number of errors made by Allan in the six months shown represented one-eighth of the total errors made by the unit during the entire year, what was the TOTAL number of errors made by the unit for the year?
   A. 124   B. 180   C. 240   D. 360

8. The number of errors made by David in November was what FRACTION of the total errors made in November?
   A. 1/3   B. 1/6   C. 3/8   D. 3/16

9. The average number of errors made per month per clerk was MOST NEARLY
   A. 4   B. 5   C. 6   D. 7

10. Of the total number of errors made during the six-month period, the percentage made in August was MOST NEARLY
    A. 2%   B. 4%   C. 23%   D. 4%

11. If the number of errors in the unit were to decrease in the next six months by 30%, what would be MOST NEARLY the total number of errors for the unit for the next six months?
    A. 87   B. 94   C. 120   D. 137

12. The arithmetic mean salary for five employees earning $18,500, $18,300, $18,600, $18,400, and $18,500, respectively is
    A. $18,450   B. $18,460   C. $18,475   D. $18,500

13. Last year, a city department which is responsible for purchasing supplies ordered bond paper in equal quantities from 22 different companies. The price was exactly the same for each company, and the total cost for the 22 orders was $693,113.
    Assuming prices did not change during the year, the cost of EACH order was MOST NEARLY
    A. $31,490   B. $31,495   C. $31,500   D. $31,505

14. A city agency engaged in repair work uses a small part which the city purchases for $0.14 each. Assume that, in a certain year, the total expenditure of the city for this part was $700.
    How MANY of these parts were purchased that year?
    A. 50   B. 200   C. 2,000   D. 5,000

15. The work unit which you supervise is responsible for processing fifteen reports per month.
    If your unit has four clerks and the best worker completes 40% of the reports himself, how many reports would each of the other clerks have to complete if they all do an equal number?
    A. 1   B. 2   C. 3   D. 4

16. Assume that the work unit in which you work has 24 clerks and 18 stenographers. In order to change the ratio of stenographers to clerks so that there is one stenographer for every four clerks, it would be necessary to REDUCE the number of stenographers by
    A. 3   B. 6   C. 9   D. 12

17. Assume that your office is responsible for opening and distributing all the mail of the division. After opening a letter, one of your subordinates notices that it states that there should be an enclosure in the envelope. However, there is no enclosure in the envelope.
    Of the following, the BEST instruction that you can give the clerk is to
    A. call the sender to obtain the enclosure
    B. call the addressee to inform him that the enclosure is missing
    C. note the omission in the margin of the letter
    D. forward the letter without taking any action

18. While opening the envelope containing official correspondence, you accidentally cut the enclosed letter.
    Of the following, the BEST action for you to take is to
    A. leave the material as it is
    B. put it together by using transparent mending tape
    C. keep it together by putting it back in the envelope
    D. keep it together by using paper clips

19. Suppose your supervisor is on the telephone in his office and an applicant arrives for a scheduled interview with him.
    Of the following, the BEST procedure to follow ordinarily is to
    A. informally chat with the applicant in your office until your supervisor has finished his phone conversation
    B. escort him directly into your supervisor's office and have him wait for him there
    C. inform your supervisor of the applicant's arrival and try to make the applicant feel comfortable while waiting
    D. have him hang up his coat and tell him to go directly in to see your supervisor

20. The length of time that files should be kept is GENERALLY
    A. considered to be seven years
    B. dependent upon how much new material has accumulated in the files
    C. directly proportionate to the number of years the office has been in operation
    D. dependent upon the type and nature of the material in the files

21. Cross-referencing a document when you file it means
    A. making a copy of the document and putting the copy into a related file
    B. indicating on the front of the document the name of the person who wrote it, the date it was written, and for what purpose
    C. putting a special sheet or card in a related file to indicate where the document is filed
    D. indicating on the document where it is to be filed

22. Unnecessary handling and recording of incoming mail could be eliminated by
    A. having the person who opens it initial it
    B. indicating on the piece of mail the names of all the individuals who should see it
    C. sending all incoming mail to more than one central location
    D. making a photocopy of each piece of incoming mail

23. Of the following, the office tasks which lend themselves MOST readily to planning and study are
    A. repetitive, occur in volume, and extend over a period of time
    B. cyclical in nature, have small volume, and extend over a short period of time
    C. tasks which occur only once in a great while not according to any schedule, and have large volume
    D. special tasks which occur only once, regardless of their volume and length of time

24. A good recordkeeping system includes all of the following procedures EXCEPT the
    A. filing of useless records
    B. destruction of certain files
    C. transferring of records from one type of file to another
    D. creation of inactive files

25. Assume that, as a supervisor, you are responsible for orienting and training new employees in your unit.
    Which of the following can MOST properly be omitted from your discussions with a new employee?
    A. The purpose of commonly used office forms
    B. Time and leave regulations
    C. Procedures for required handling of routine business calls
    D. The reason the last employee was fired

KEY (CORRECT ANSWERS)

1.	A	11.	A
2.	D	12.	B
3.	B	13.	D
4.	B	14.	D
5.	A	15.	C
6.	C	16.	D
7.	C	17.	C
8.	C	18.	B
9.	B	19.	C
10.	C	20.	D

21. C
22. B
23. A
24. A
25. D

READING COMPREHENSION
UNDERSTANDING AND INTERPRETING WRITTEN MATERIAL
EXAMINATION SECTION
TEST 1

DIRECTIONS: All questions are to be answered SOLELY on the basis of the information contained in the passage. Each question or incomplete statement is followed by several suggested answers or completions. Select the one that BEST answers the question or completes the statement. *PRINT THE LETTER OF THE CORRECT ANSWER IN THE SPACE AT THE RIGHT.*

Questions 1-7.

Snow-covered roads spell trouble for motorists all winter long. Clearing highways of snow and ice to keep millions of motor vehicles moving freely is a tremendous task. Highway departments now rely, to a great extent, on chemical de-icers to get the big job done. Sodium chloride, in the form of commercial salt, is the de-icer most frequently used.

There is no reliable evidence to prove that salt reduces highway accidents. But available statistics are impressive. For example, before Massachusetts used chemical de-icers, it had a yearly average of 21 fatal accidents and 1,635 injuries attributed to cars skidding on snow or ice. Beginning in 1990, the state began fighting hazardous driving conditions with chemical de-icers. During the period 1990-2000, there was a yearly average of only seven deaths and 736 injuries as a result of skids.

Economical and effective in a moderately low temperature range, salt is increasingly popular with highway departments, but not so popular with individual car owners. Salty slush eats away at metal, including auto bodies. It also sprinkles windshields with a fine-grained spray which dries on contact, severely reducing visibility. However, drivers who are hindered or immobilized by heavy winter weather favor the liberal use of products such as sodium chloride. When snow blankets roads, these drivers feel that the quickest way to get back to the safety of driving on bare pavement is through use of de-icing salts.

1. The MAIN reason given by the above passage for the use of sodium chloride as a de-icer is that it
    A. has no harmful effects
    B. is economical
    C. is popular among car owners
    D. reduces highway accidents

1.____

2. The above passage may BEST be described as a(n)
    A. argument against the use of sodium chloride as a de-icer
    B. discussion of some advantages and disadvantages of sodium chloride as a de-icer
    C. recommendation to use sodium chloride as a de-icer
    D. technical account of the uses and effects of sodium chloride as a de-icer

2.____

3. Based on the above passage, the use of salt on snow-covered roadways will eventually
   A. decrease the efficiency of the automobile fuel
   B. cause tires to deteriorate
   C. damage the surface of the roadway
   D. cause holes in the sides of cars

4. The average number of persons killed yearly in Massachusetts in car accidents caused by skidding on snow or ice, before chemical de-icers were used there, was
   A. 9 B. 12 C. 21 D. 30

5. According to the above passage, it would be advisable to use salt as a de-icer when
   A. outdoor temperatures are somewhat below freezing
   B. residues on highway surfaces are deemed to be undesirable
   C. snow and ice have low absorbency characteristics
   D. the use of a substance is desired which dries on contact

6. As a result of using chemical de-icers, the number of injuries resulting from skids in Massachusetts was reduced by about
   A. 35% B. 45% C. 55% D. 65%

7. According to the above passage, driver visibility can be severely reduced by
   A. sodium chloride deposits on the windshield
   B. glare from salt and snow crystals
   C. salt spray covering the front lights
   D. faulty windshield wipers

Questions 8-10.

An employee should call the Fire Department for any fire except a small one in a wastebasket. This kind of fire can be put out with a fire extinguisher. If the employee is not sure about the size of the fire, he should not wait to find out how big it is. He should call the Fire Department at once.
Every employee should know what to do when a fire starts. He should know how to use the firefighting tools in the building and how to call the Fire Department. He should also know where the nearest fire alarm box is. But the most important thing for an employee to do in case of fire is to avoid panic.

8. If there is a small fire in a wastebasket, an employee should
   A. call the Fire Department   B. let it burn itself out
   C. open a window   D. put it out with a fire extinguisher

9. In case of fire, the MOST important thing for an employee to do is to
   A. find out how big it is   B. keep calm
   C. leave the building right away D. report to his boss

10. If a large fire starts while he is at work, an employee should always FIRST
    A. call the Fire Department
    B. notify the Housing Superintendent
    C. remove inflammables from the building
    D. use a fire extinguisher

Questions 11-12.

Those correction theorists who are in agreement with severe and rigid controls as a normal part of the correctional process are confronted with a contradiction; this is so because a responsibility which is consistent with freedom cannot be developed in a repressive atmosphere. They do not recognize this contradiction when they carry out their programs with dictatorial force and expect convicted criminals exposed to such programs to be reformed into free and responsible citizens.

11. According to the above passage, those correction theorists are faced with a contradiction who
    A. are in favor of the enforcement of strict controls in a prison
    B. believe that to develop a sense of responsibility, freedom must not be restricted
    C. take the position that the development of responsibility consistent with freedom is not possible in a repressive atmosphere
    D. think that freedom and responsibility can be developed only in a democratic atmosphere

12. According to the above passage, a repressive atmosphere in a prison
    A. does not conform to present-day ideas of freedom of the individual
    B. is admitted by correction theorists to be in conflict with the basic principles of the normal correctional process
    C. is advocated as the best method of maintaining discipline when rehabilitation is of secondary importance
    D. is not suitable for the development of a sense of responsibility consistent with freedom

Questions 13-16.

Abandoned cars—with tires gone, chrome stripped away, and windows smashed—have become a common sight on the City's streets. In 2020, more than 72,000 were deposited at curbs by owners who never came back, an increase of 15,000 from the year before and more than 30 times the number abandoned a decade ago. In January, 2021, the City's Environmental Protection Administrator asked the State Legislature to pass a law requiring a buyer of a new automobile to deposit $100 and an owner of an automobile at the time the law takes effect to deposit $50 with the State Department of Motor Vehicles. In return, they would be given a certificate of deposit which would be passed on to each succeeding owner. The final owner would get the deposit money back if he could present proof that he has disposed of his car "in an environmentally acceptable manner." The Legislature has given no indication that it plans to rush ahead on the matter.

4 (#1)

13. The number of cars abandoned in City streets in 2010 was MOST NEARLY   13._____
    A. 2,500   B. 12,000   C. 27,500   D. 57,000

14. The proposed law would require a person who owned a car bought before the   14._____
    law was passed to deposit
    A. $100 with the State Department of Motor Vehicles
    B. $50 with the Environmental Protection Administration
    C. $100 with the State Legislature
    D. $50 with the State Department of Motor Vehicles

15. The proposed law would require the State to return the deposit money only   15._____
    when the
    A. original owner of the car shows roof that he sold it
    B. last owner of the car shows proof that he got rid of the car in a
       satisfactory way
    C. owner of the car shows proof that he has transferred the certificate of
       deposit to the next owner
    D. last owner of a car returns the certificate of deposit

16. The MAIN idea or theme of the above article is that   16._____
    A. a proposed new law would make it necessary for car owners in the State
       to pay additional taxes
    B. the State Legislature is against a proposed law to require deposits from
       automobile owners to prevent them from abandoning their cars
    C. the City is trying to find a solution for the increasing number of cars
       abandoned on its streets
    D. to pay for the removal of abandoned cars, the City's Environmental
       Protection Administrator has asked the State to fine automobile owners
       who abandon their vehicles

Questions 17-19.

The German roach is the most common roach in houses in the United State. Adults are pale brown and about ½-inch long; both sexes have wings as long as the body, and can be distinguished from other roaches by the two dark stripes on the pronotum. The female carries its egg capsule protruding from her abdomen until the eggs are ready to hatch. This is the only common house-infesting species which carries the egg capsule for such an extended period of time. A female will usually produce 4 to 8 capsules in her lifetime. Each capsule contains 30 to 48 eggs which hatch out in about 28 days at ordinary room temperature. The completion of the nymph stage under room conditions requires 40 to 125 days. German roaches may live as adults for as long as 303 days.

It is stated about that the German cockroach is the most commonly encountered of the house-infesting species in the United States. The reasons for this are somewhat complex, but the understanding of some of the factors involved are basic to the practice of pest control. In the first place, the German cockroach has a larger number of eggs per capsule and a shorter hatching time than do the other species. It also requires a shorter period from hatching until sexual maturity, so that within a given period of time a population of German roaches will produce a larger number of eggs. Onn the basis of this fact, we can state that this species has a high reproductive potential. Since the female carries the egg capsule during nearly the entire time that the embryos are developing within the egg, many hazards of the environment which may affect the eggs are avoided. This means that more nymphs are likely to hatch and that a larger portion of the reproductive potential is realized. The nymphs which hatch from each egg capsule tend to stay close to each other, and since they are often close to the female at time of hatching, there is a tendency for the population density to be high locally. Being smaller than most of the other roaches, they are able to conceal themselves in many places which are inaccessible to individuals of the larger species. All of these factors combined help to give the German cockroach an advantage with regard to group survival.

17. According to the above passage, the MOST important feature of the German roach which gives it an advantage over other roaches is
    A. distinctive markings
    B. immunity to disease
    C. long life span
    D. power to reproduce

    17._____

18. An IMPORTANT difference between an adult female German roach and an adult female of other species is the
    A. black bars or stripes which appear on the abdomen of the German roach
    B. German roach's preference for warm, moist places in which to breed
    C. long period of time during which the German roach carries the egg capsule
    D. presence of longer wings on the female German roach

    18._____

19. A storeroom in a certain housing project has an infestation of German roaches, which includes 125 adult female.
    If the infestation is not treated and ordinary room temperature is maintained in the storeroom, how many eggs will hatch out during the lifetime of these females if they each lay 8 capsules containing 48 eggs each?
    A. 1,500   B. 48,000   C. 96,000   D. 303,000

    19._____

Questions 20-22.

City governments have long had building codes which set minimum standards for building and for human occupancy. The code (or series of codes) makes provisions for standards of lighting and ventilation, sanitation, fire prevention, and protection. As a result of demands from manufacturers, builders, real estate people, tenement owners, and building-trades unions, these codes often have established minimum standards well below those that the contemporary society would accept as a rock-bottom minimum. Codes often become outdated, so that meager standards in one era become seriously inadequate a few decades later as society's concept of a minimum standard of living changes. Out-of-date codes, when still in use, have sometimes prevented the introduction of new devices and modern building techniques. Thus, it is extremely important that building codes keep pace with changes in the accepted concept of a minimum standard of living.

20. According to the above passage, all of the following considerations in building planning would probably be covered in a building code EXCEPT
    A. closet space as a percentage of total floor area
    B. size and number of windows required for rooms of differing sizes

    20._____

C. placement of fire escapes in each line of apartments
D. type of garbage disposal units to be installed

21. According to the above passage, if an ideal building code were to be created, how would the established minimum standards in it compare to the ones that are presently set by city governments?
They would
   A. be lower than they are at present
   B. be higher than they are at present
   C. be comparable to the present minimum standards
   D. vary according to the economic group that sets them

22. On the basis of the above passage, what is the reason for difficulties in introducing new building techniques?
   A. Builders prefer techniques which represent the rock-bottom minimum desired by society.
   B. Certain manufacturers have obtained patents on various building methods to the exclusion of new techniques.
   C. The government does not want to invest money in techniques that will soon be outdated.
   D. New techniques are not provided for in building codes which are not up-to-date.

Questions 23-25.

A flameproof fabric is defined as one which, when exposed to small sources of ignition such as sparks or smoldering cigarettes, does not burn beyond the vicinity of the source of the ignition. Cotton fabrics are the materials commonly used that are considered most hazardous. Other materials, such as acetate rayons and linens, are somewhat less hazardous, and woolens and some natural silk fabrics, even when untreated, are about the equal of the average treated cotton fabric insofar as flame spread and ease of ignition are concerned. The method of application is to immerse the fabric in a flameproofing solution. The container used must be large enough so that all the fabric is thoroughly wet and there are no folds which the solution does not penetrate.

23. According to the above passage, a flameproof fabric is one which
   A. is unaffected by heat and smoke
   B. resists the spread of flames when ignited
   C. burns with a cold flame
   D. cannot be ignited by sparks or cigarettes
   E. may smolder but cannot burn

24. According to the above passage, woolen fabrics which have not been flameproofed are as likely to catch fire as _____ fabrics.
   A. treated silk   B. treated acetate rayon
   C. untreated linen   D. untreated synthetic
   E. treated cotton

25. In the method described above, the flameproofing solution is BEST applied to the fabric by _____ the fabric.   25._____
    A. sponging
    B. spraying
    C. dipping
    D. brushing
    E. sprinkling

KEY (CORRECT ANSWERS)

1.	B	11.	A
2.	B	12.	D
3.	D	13.	A
4.	C	14.	D
5.	A	15.	B
6.	C	16.	C
7.	A	17.	D
8.	D	18.	C
9.	B	19.	B
10.	A	20.	A

21. B
22. D
23. B
24. E
25. C

TEST 2

DIRECTIONS: All questions are to be answered SOLELY on the basis of the information contained in the passage. Each question or incomplete statement is followed by several suggested answers or completions. Select the one that BEST answers the question or completes the statement. *PRINT THE LETTER OF THE CORRECT ANSWER IN THE SPACE AT THE RIGHT.*

Questions 1-4.

Safety belts provide protection for the passengers of a vehicle by preventing them from crashing around inside if the vehicle is involved in a collision. They operate on the principle similar to that used in the packaging of fragile items. You become a part of the vehicle package and you are kept from being tossed about inside if the vehicle is suddenly decelerated. Many injury-causing collisions at low speeds—for example, at city intersections—could have been injury-free if the occupants had fastened their safety belts. There is a double advantage to the driver in that it not only protects him from harm, but prevents him from being yanked away from the wheel, thereby permitting him to maintain control of the car. Since, without seat belts, the risk of injury is about 50% greater, and the risk of death is about 30% greater, the State Vehicle and Traffic Law provided that a motor vehicle manufactured or assembled after June 30, 1964 and designated as a 1965 or later model should have two safety belts for the front seat. It also provides that a motor vehicle manufactured after June 30, 1966 and designated as a 1967 or later model should have at least one safety belt for the rear seat for each passenger for which the rear seat of such vehicle was designed.

1. The principle on which seat belts work is that
    A. a car and its driver and passengers are fragile
    B. a person fastened to the car will not be thrown around when the car slows down suddenly
    C. the driver and passengers of a car that is suddenly decelerated will be thrown forward
    D. the driver and passengers of an automobile should be packaged the way fragile items are packaged

2. We can assume from the above passage that safety belts should be worn at all times because you can never tell when
    A. a car will be forced to turn off onto another road
    B. it will be necessary to shift into low gear to go up a hill
    C. you will have to speed up to pass another car
    D. a car may have to come to a sudden stop

3. Besides preventing injury, an ADDITIONAL benefit from the use of safety belts is that
    A. collisions are fewer
    B. damage to the car is kept down
    C. the car can be kept under control
    D. the number of accidents at city intersections is reduced

4. The risk of death in car accidents for people who don't use safety belts is
   A. 30% greater than the risk of injury
   B. 30% greater than for those who do use them
   C. 50% less than the risk of injury
   D. 50% greater than for those who use them

Questions 5-9.

Any person who is living in New York City and is otherwise eligible may be granted public assistance whether or not he has New York State residence. However, since New York City does not contribute to the cost of assistance granted to persons who are without State residence, the cases of all recipients must be formally identified as to whether or not each member of the household has State residence.

To acquire State residence a person must have resided in New York State continuously for one year. Such residence is not lost unless the person is out of the State continuously for a period of one year or longer. Continuous residence does not include any period during which the individual is a patient in a hospital, an inmate of a public institution or of an incorporated private institution, a resident on a military reservation, or a minor residing in a boarding home while under the care of an authorized agency. Receipt of public assistance does not prevent a person from acquiring State residence. State residence, once acquired, is not lost because of absence from the State while a person is serving in the U.S. Armed Forces or the Merchant Marine; nor does a member of the family of such a person lose State residence while living with or near that person in these circumstances.

Each person, regardless of age, acquires or loses State residence as an individual. There is no derivative State residence except for an infant at the time of birth. He is deemed to have State residence if he is in the custody of both parents and either one of them has State residence, or if the parent having custody of him has State residence.

5. According to the above passage, an infant is deemed to have New York State residence at the time of his birth if
   A. he is born in New York State but neither of his parents is a resident
   B. he is in custody of only one parent, who is not a resident, but his other parent is a resident
   C. his brother and sister are residents
   D. he is in the custody of both his parents but only one of them is a resident

6. The Jones family consists of five members. Jack and Mary Jones have lived in New York State continuously for the past eighteen months after having lived in Ohio since they were born. Of their three children, one was born ten months ago and has been in custody of his parents since birth. Their second child lived in Ohio until six months ago and then moved in with his parents. Their third child had never lived in New York until he moved with his parents to New York eighteen months ago. However, he entered the armed forces one month later and has not lived in New York since that time.
Based on the above passage, how many members of the Jones Family are New York State residents?
   A. 2   B. 3   C. 4   D. 5

7. Assuming that each of the following individuals has lived continuously in New York State for the past year and has never previously lived in the State, which one of them is a New York State resident?
   A. Jack Salinas, who has been an inmate in a State correctional facility for six months of the year
   B. Fran Johnson, who has lived on an Army base for the entire year
   C. Arlene Snyder, who married a non-resident during the past year
   D. Gary Phillips, who was a patient in a Veterans Administration hospital for the entire year

8. The above passage implies that the reason for determining whether or not a recipient of public assistance is a State resident is that
   A. the cost of assistance for non-residents is not a New York City responsibility
   B. non-residents living in New York City are not eligible for public assistance
   C. recipients of public assistance are barred from acquiring State residence
   D. New York City is responsible for the full cost of assistance to recipients who are residents

9. Assume that the Rollins household in New York City consists of six members at the present time—Anne Rollins, her three children, her aunt, and her uncle. Anne Rollins and one of her children moved to New York City seven months ago. Neither of them had previously lived in New York State. Her other two children have lived in New York City continuously for the past two years, as has her aunt. Anne Rollins' uncle had lived in New York City continuously for many years until two years ago. He then entered the armed forces and has returned to New York City within the past month.
   Based on the above passage, how many members of the Rollins' household are New York State residents?
   A. 2   B. 3   C. 4   D. 6

Questions 10-12.

The agreement under which a tenant rents property from a landlord is known as a lease. Generally speaking, leases are classified as either short-term or long-term in duration. They are further subdivided according to the method used to determine the amount of periodic rent payments. Of the many types of lease in use, the more commonly used ones are the following:
   1. The straight or fixed lease is one in which rent may be paid in equal amounts throughout the duration of the lease. These are usually restricted to short-term leasing, or somewhat longer-term if clauses in the lease provide for periodic escalation of payments as the economy shifts.
   2. Percentage leasing, used for short-term commercial leasing, provides the landlord with a stipulated percentage of a tenant's gross sales from goods and services sold on the premises, in addition to a fixed amount of rent.
   3. The net lease, generally long-term (ten years or more), requires the tenant to pay all operating costs, including real estate taxes and insurance. In a net-net lease, the tenant further agrees to meet mortgage interest and principal payments.

4. An escalated lease, which is a long-term lease, requires rent to be of a stipulated base amount which periodically is subject to escalation in accordance with cost-of-living index scales, or in direct proportion to taxes, insurance, and operating costs.

10. Based on the information given in the above passage, which type of lease is MOST likely to be advantageous to a landlord if there is a high rate of inflation?   10.____
    A. Fixed lease
    B. Percentage lease
    C. Net lease
    D. Escalated lease

11. On the basis of the above passage, which type of lease would generally be MOST suitable for a well-established textile company which requires permanent facilities for its large operations?   11.____
    A. Percentage lease and escalated lease
    B. Escalated lease and net lease
    C. Straight lease and net lease
    D. Straight lease and percentage lease

12. According to the above passage, the only type of lease which assures the same amount of rent throughout a specified interval is the _____ lease.   12.____
    A. straight   B. percentage   C. net-net   D. escalated

Questions 13-18.

Basic to every office is the need for proper lighting. Inadequate lighting is a familiar cause of fatigue and serves to create a somewhat dismal atmosphere in the office. One requirement of proper lighting is that it be an appropriate intensity. Intensity is measured in foot-candles. According to the Illuminating Engineering Society of New York, for casual seeing tasks such as in reception rooms, inactive file rooms, and other service areas, it is recommended that the amount of light be 30 foot-candles. For ordinary seeing tasks such as reading and work in active file rooms and in mail rooms, the recommended lighting is 100 foot-candles. For very difficult seeing tasks such as accounting, transcribing, and business-machine use, the recommended lighting is 150 foot-candles.

Lighting intensity is only one requirement. Shadows and glare are to be avoided. For example, the larger the proportion of a ceiling filled with lighting units, the more glare-free and comfortable the lighting will be. Natural lighting from windows is not too dependable because on dark wintry days windows yield little usable light, and on sunny, summer afternoons the glare from windows may be very distracting. Desks should not face the windows. Finally, the main lighting source ought to be overhead and to the left of the user.

13. According to the above passage, insufficient light in the office may cause   13.____
    A. glare   B. shadows   C. tiredness   D. distraction

14. Based on the above passage, which of the following must be considered when planning lighting arrangements? The   14.____
    A. amount of natural light present
    B. amount of work to be done
    C. level of difficulty of work to be done
    D. type of activity to be carried out

15. It can be inferred from the above passage that a well-coordinated lighting scheme is likely to result in
    A. greater employee productivity
    B. elimination of light reflection
    C. lower lighting cost
    D. more use of natural light

15.____

16. Of the following, the BEST title for the above passage is:
    A. Characteristics of Light
    B. Light Measurement Devices
    C. Factors to Consider When Planning Lighting Systems
    D. Comfort vs. Cost When Devising Lighting Arrangements

16.____

17. According to the above passage, a foot-candle is a measurement of the
    A. number of bulbs used
    B. strength of the light
    C. contrast between glare and shadow
    D. proportion of the ceiling filled with lighting units

17.____

18. According to the above passage, the number of foot-candles of light that would be needed to copy figures onto a payroll is _____ foot-candles.
    A. less than 30   B. 350   C. 100   D. 140

18.____

Questions 19-22.

A summons is an official statement ordering a person to appear in court. In traffic violation situations, summonses are used when arrests need not be made. The main reason for traffic summonses is to deter motorists from repeating the same traffic violation. Occasionally, motorists may make unintentional driving errors and sometimes they are unaware of correct driving regulations. In cases such as these, the policy should be to have the Officer verbally inform the motorist of the violation and warn him against repeating it. The purpose of this practice is not to limit the number of summonses, but rather to prevent the issuing of summonses when the violation is not due to deliberate intent or to inexcusable negligence.

19. According to the above passage, the PRINCIPAL reason for issuing traffic summonses is to
    A. discourage motorists from violating these laws again
    B. increase the money collected by the city
    C. put traffic violators in prison
    D. have them serve as substitutes for police officers

19.____

20. The reason a verbal warning may sometimes be substituted for a summons is to
    A. limit the number of summonses
    B. distinguish between excusable and inexcusable violations
    C. provide harsher penalties for deliberate intent than for inexcusable negligence
    D. decrease the caseload in the courts

20.____

21. The author of the above passage feels that someone who violated a traffic regulation because he did not know about the regulation should be
    A. put under arrest
    B. fined less money
    C. given a summons
    D. told not to do it again

22. Using the distinctions made by the author of the above passage, the one of the following motorists to whom it would be MOST desirable to issue a summons is the one who exceeded the speed limit because he
    A. did not know the speed limit
    B. was late for an important business appointment
    C. speeded to avoid being hit by another car
    D. had a speedometer which was not working properly

Questions 24-25.

Physical design plays a very significant role in crime rate. Crime rate has been found to increase almost proportionately with building height. The average number of crimes is much greater in higher buildings than in lower ones (equal to or less than six stories). What is most interesting is that in buildings of six stories or less, the project size or total number of units does not make a difference. It seems that, although larger projects encourage crime by fostering feelings of anonymity, isolation, irresponsibility, and lack of identity with surroundings, evidence indicate that larger projects encompassed in low buildings seem to offset what we may assume to be factors conducive to high crime rates. High-rise projects not only experience a higher rate of crime within the buildings, but a greater proportion of the crime occurs in the interior public spaces of these buildings as compared with those of the lower buildings. Lower buildings have more limited public space than higher ones. A criminal probably perceives that the interior public areas of buildings are where his victims are most vulnerable and where the possibility of his being seen or apprehended is minimal. Placement of elevators, entrance lobbies, and secondary exits all are factors related to the likelihood of crimes taking place in buildings. The study of all of these elements should bear some weight in the planning of new projects.

23. According to the above passage, which of the following BEST describes the relationship between building size and crime?
    A. Larger projects lead to a greater crime rate.
    B. Higher buildings tend to increase the crime rate.
    C. The smaller the number of project apartments in low buildings the higher the crime rate
    D. Anonymity and isolation serve to lower the crime rate in small buildings.

24. According to the above passage, the likelihood of a criminal attempting a mugging in the interior public portions of a high-rise building is good because
    A. tenants will be constantly flowing in and out of the area
    B. there is easy access to fire stairs and secondary exits
    C. there is a good chance that no one will see him
    D. tenants may not recognize the victims of crime as their neighbors

25. Which of the following is *implied* by the above passage as an explanation for the fact that the crime rate is lower in large low-rise housing projects than in large high-rise projects?
    A. Tenants know each other better and take a greater interest in what happens in the project.
    B. There is more public space where tenants are likely to gather together.
    C. The total number of units in a low-rise project is fewer than the total number of units in a high-rise project.
    D. Elevators in low-rise buildings travel quickly, thus limiting the amount of time in which a criminal can act.

25._____

KEY (CORRECT ANSWERS)

1.	B		11.	B
2.	D		12.	A
3.	C		13.	C
4.	B		14.	D
5.	D		15.	A
6.	B		16.	C
7.	C		17.	B
8.	A		18.	D
9.	C		19.	A
10.	D		20.	B

21.	D
22.	B
23.	B
24.	C
25.	A

EXAMINATION SECTION
TEST 1

DIRECTIONS: In each of the following tests in this part, select the letter of the one MIS-SPELLED word in each of the following groups of words. If no word is misspelled, select the last item, letter E (none misspelled). *PRINT THE LETTER OF THE CORRECT ANSWER IN THE SPACE AT THE RIGHT.*

1. A. grateful   B. fundimental   C. census   1._____
   D. analysis   E. NONE MISSPELLED

2. A. installment   B. retrieve   C. concede   2._____
   D. dissapear   E. NONE MISSPELLED

3. A. accidentaly   B. dismissal   C. conscientious   3._____
   D. indelible   E. NONE MISSPELLED

4. A. perceive   B. carreer   C. anticipate   4._____
   D. acquire   E. NONE MISSPELLED

5. A. facility   B. reimburse   C. assortment   5._____
   D. guidance   E. NONE MISSPELLED

6. A. plentiful   B. across   C. advantagous   6._____
   D. similar   E. NONE MISSPELLED

7. A. omission   B. pamphlet   C. guarrantee   7._____
   D. repel   E. NONE MISSPELLED

8. A. maintenance   B. always   C. liable   8._____
   D. anouncement   E. NONE MISSPELLED

9. A. exaggerate   B. sieze   C. condemn   9._____
   D. commit   E. NONE MISSPELLED

10. A. pospone   B. altogether   C. grievance   10._____
    D. excessive   E. NONE MISSPELLED

11. A. arguing   B. correspondance   C. forfeit   11._____
    D. dissension   E. NONE MISSPELLED

12. A. occasion   B. description   C. prejudice   12._____
    D. elegible   E. NONE MISSPELLED

13. A. accomodate   B. initiative   C. changeable   13._____
    D. enroll   E. NONE MISSPELLED

14. A. temporary   B. insistent   C. benificial   14._____
    D. separate   E. NONE MISSPELLED

15. A. achieve   B. dissapoint   C. unanimous   15._____
    D. judgment   E. NONE MISSPELLED

16. A. proceed   B. publicly   C. sincerity   16._____
    D. successful   E. NONE MISSPELLED

17. A. deceive   B. goverment   C. preferable   17._____
    D. repetitive   E. *NONE MISSPELLED*

18. A. emphasis   B. skillful   C. advisible   18._____
    D. optimistic   E. *NONE MISSPELLED*

19. A. tendency   B. rescind   C. crucial   19._____
    D. noticable   E. *NONE MISSPELLED*

20. A. privelege   B. abbreviate   C. simplify   20._____
    D. divisible   E. *NONE MISSPELLED*

KEY (CORRECT ANSWERS)

1. B. fundamental
2. D. disappear
3. A. accidentally
4. B. career
5. E. None Misspelled
6. C. advantageous
7. C. guarantee
8. D. announcement
9. B. seize
10. A. postpone
11. B. correspondence
12. D. eligible
13. A. accommodate
14. C. beneficial
15. B. disappoint
16. E. None Misspelled
17. B. government
18. C. advisable
19. D. noticeable
20. A. privilege

TEST 2

DIRECTIONS: In each of the following tests in this part, select the letter of the one MIS-SPELLED word in each of the following groups of words. If no word is misspelled, select the last item, letter E (none misspelled). *PRINT THE LETTER OF THE CORRECT ANSWER IN THE SPACE AT THE RIGHT.*

1. A. typical B. descend C. summarize 1.____
   D. continuel E. *NONE MISSPELLED*

2. A. courageous B. recomend C. omission 2.____
   D. eliminate E. *NONE MISSPELLED*

3. A. compliment B. illuminate C. auxilary 3.____
   D. installation E. *NONE MISSPELLED*

4. A. preliminary B. aquainted C. syllable 4.____
   D. analysis E. *NONE MISSPELLED*

5. A. accustomed B. negligible C. interupted 5.____
   D. bulletin E. *NONE MISSPELLED*

6. A. summoned B. managment C. mechanism 6.____
   D. sequence E. *NONE MISSPELLED*

7. A. commitee B. surprise C. noticeable 7.____
   D. emphasize E. *NONE MISSPELLED*

8. A. occurrance B. likely C. accumulate 8.____
   D. grievance E. grievance

9. A. obstacle B. particuliar C. baggage 9.____
   D. fascinating E. *NONE MISSPELLED*

10. A. innumerable B. seize C. applicant 10.____
    D. dicionery E. *NONE MISSPELLED*

11. A. primary B. mechanic C. referred 11.____
    D. admissible E. *NONE MISSPELLED*

12. A. cessation B. beleif C. aggressive 12.____
    D. allowance E. *NONE MISSPELLED*

13. A. leisure B. authentic C. familiar 13.____
    D. contemptable E. *NONE MISSPELLED*

14. A. volume B. forty C. dilemma 14.____
    D. seldum E. *NONE MISSPELLED*

15. A. discrepancy B. aquisition C. exorbitant 15.____
    D. lenient E. *NONE MISSPELLED*

16. A. simultanous B. penetrate C. revision 16.____
    D. conspicuous E. *NONE MISSPELLED*

17. A. ilegible B. gracious C. profitable 17.____
    D. obedience E. *NONE MISSPELLED*

69

18. A. manufacturer   B. authorize   C. compelling   18.____
    D. pecular   E. *NONE MISSPELLED*

19. A. anxious   B. rehearsal   C. handicaped   19.____
    D. tendency   E. *NONE MISSPELLED*

20. A. meticulous   B. accompaning C. initiative   20.____
    D. shelves   E. *NONE MISSPELLED*

KEY (CORRECT ANSWERS)

1. D. continual
2. B. recommend
3. C. auxiliary
4. B. acquainted
5. C. interrupted
6. B. management
7. A. committee
8. A. occurrence
9. B. particular
10. D. dictionary
11. E. None Misspelled
12. B. belief
13. D. contemptible
14. D. seldom
15. B. acquisition
16. A. simultaneous
17. A. illegible
18. D. peculiar
19. C. handicapped
20. B. accompanying

TEST 3

DIRECTIONS: In each of the following tests in this part, select the letter of the one MIS-SPELLED word in each of the following groups of words. If no word is misspelled, select the last item, letter E (none misspelled). *PRINT THE LETTER OF THE CORRECT ANSWER IN THE SPACE AT THE RIGHT.*

1. A. grievous B. dilettante C. gibberish 1.____
   D. upbraid E. *NONE MISSPELLED*

2. A. embarrassing B. playright C. unmanageable 2.____
   D. symmetrical E. *NONE MISSPELLED*

3. A. sestet B. denouement C. liaison 3.____
   D. tattooing E. *NONE MISSPELLED*

4. A. prophesied B. soliliquy C. supersede 4.____
   D. hemorrhage E. *NONE MISSPELLED*

5. A. colossal B. renascent C. parallel 5.____
   D. omnivorous E. *NONE MISSPELLED*

6. A. passable B. dispensable C. deductable 6.____
   D. irreducible E. *NONE MISSPELLED*

7. A. guerrila B. carousal C. maneuver 7.____
   D. staid E. *NONE MISSPELLED*

8. A. maintenance B. mountainous C. sustenance 8.____
   D. gluttinous E. *NONE MISSPELLED*

9. A. holocaust B. irascible C. buccanneer 9.____
   D. mischievous E. *NONE MISSPELLED*

10. A. diphthong B. rhododendron C. inviegle 10.____
    D. shellacked E. *NONE MISSPELLED*

11. A. Phillipines B. currant C. dietitian 11.____
    D. coercion E. *NONE MISSPELLED*

12. A. courtesey B. buoyancy C. fiery 12.____
    D. shepherd E. *NONE MISSPELLED*

13. A. censor B. queue C. obbligato 13.____
    D. antartic E. *NONE MISSPELLED*

14. A. chrystal B. chrysanthemum C. chrysalis 14.____
    D. chrome E. *NONE MISSPELLED*

15. A. shreik B. siege C. sheik 15.____
    D. sieve E. *NONE MISSPELLED*

16. A. leisure B. gladioluses C. kindergarden 16.____
    D. tonnage E. *NONE MISSPELLED*

17. A. emminent B. imminent C. blatant 17.____
    D. privilege E. *NONE MISSPELLED*

18.	A. diphtheria D. sleight	B. collander E. *NONE MISSPELLED*	C. seize	18.____
19.	A. frolicking D. kohlrabi	B. caramel E. *NONE MISSPELLED*	C. germaine	19.____
20.	A. dispensable D. feasible	B. compatable E. *NONE MISSPELLED*	C. recommend	20.____

KEY (CORRECT ANSWERS)

1. E. None Misspelled
2. B. playwright
3. E. None Misspelled
4. B. soliloquy
5. E. None Misspelled
6. C. deductible
7. A. guerrilla
8. D. gluttonous
9. C. buccaneer
10. C. inveigle
11. A. Philippines
12. A. courtesy
13. D. antarctic
14. A. crystal
15. A. shriek
16. C. kindergarten
17. A. eminent
18. B. colander
19. C. germane
20. B. compatible

TEST 4

DIRECTIONS: In each of the following tests in this part, select the letter of the one MISSPELLED word in each of the following groups of words. If no word is misspelled, select the last item, letter E (none misspelled). *PRINT THE LETTER OF THE CORRECT ANSWER IN THE SPACE AT THE RIGHT.*

1. A. coercion B. rescission C. license 1.____
   D. prophecied E. *NONE MISSPELLED*

2. A. calcimine B. seive C. procedure 2.____
   D. poinsettia E. *NONE MISSPELLED*

3. A. entymology B. echoing C. subtly 3.____
   D. stupefy E. *NONE MISSPELLED*

4. A. mocassin B. assassin C. battalion 4.____
   D. despicable E. *NONE MISSPELLED*

5. A. moustache B. sovereignty C. drunkeness 5.____
   D. staccato E. *NONE MISSPELLED*

6. A. notoriety B. stereotype C. trellis 6.____
   D. Uraguay E. *NONE MISSPELLED*

7. A. hummock B. idiosyncrasy C. licentiate 7.____
   D. plagiarism E. *NONE MISSPELLED*

8. A. denim B. hyssop C. innoculate 8.____
   D. malevolent E. *NONE MISSPELLED*

9. A. boundaries B. corpulency C. gauge 9.____
   D. jingoes E. *NONE MISSPELLED*

10. A. assassin B. refulgeant C. sorghum 10.____
    D. suture E. *NONE MISSPELLED*

11. A. dormatory B. glimpse C. mediocre 11.____
    D. repetition E. *NONE MISSPELLED*

12. A. ambergris B. docility C. loquacious 12.____
    D. Pharoah E. *NONE MISSPELLED*

13. A. curriculum B. ninety-eighth C. occurrence 13.____
    D. repertoire E. *NONE MISSPELLED*

14. A. belladonna B. equable C. immersion 14.____
    D. naphtha E. *NONE MISSPELLED*

15. A. itinerary B. ptomaine C. similar 15.____
    D. solicetous E. *NONE MISSPELLED*

16. A. liquify B. mausoleum C. Philippines 16.____
    D. singeing E. *NONE MISSPELLED*

17. A. descendant B. harrassed C. implausible 17.____
    D. irreverence E. *NONE MISSPELLED*

18. A. crystallize B. imperceptible C. isinglass 18.____
    D. precede E. *NONE MISSPELLED*

19. A. accommodate B. deferential C. gazeteer 19.____
    D. plenteous E. *NONE MISSPELLED*

20. A. aching B. buttress C. indigenous 20.____
    D. mischievous E. *NONE MISSPELLED*

KEY (CORRECT ANSWERS)

1. D. prophesied
2. B. sieve
3. A. entomology
4. A. moccasin
5. C. drunkenness
6. D. Uruguay
7. E. None Misspelled
8. C. inoculate
9. E. None Misspelled
10. B. refulgent
11. A. dormitory
12. D. Pharaoh
13. E. None Misspelled
14. E. None misspelled
15. D. solicitous
16. A. liquefy
17. B. harassed
18. E. None Misspelled
19. C. gazetteer
20. E. None Misspelled

TEST 5

DIRECTIONS: In each of the following tests in this part, select the letter of the one MIS-SPELLED word in each of the following groups of words. If no word is misspelled, select the last item, letter E (none misspelled). *PRINT THE LETTER OF THE CORRECT ANSWER IN THE SPACE AT THE RIGHT.*

1. A. comensurable   B. fracas   C. obeisance   1.____
   D. remittent   E. NONE MISSPELLED

2. A. defiance   B. delapidated   C. motley   2.____
   D. rueful   E. NONE MISSPELLED

3. A. demeanor   B. epoch   C. furtive   3.____
   D. parley   E. NONE MISSPELLED

4. A. disciples   B. influencial   C. nemesis   4.____
   D. poultry   E. NONE MISSPELLED

5. A. decision   B. encourage   C. incidental   5.____
   D. satyr   E. NONE MISSPELLED

6. A. collate   B. connivance   C. luxurient   6.____
   D. manageable   E. NONE MISSPELLED

7. A. constituencies   B. crocheted   C. foreclosure   7.____
   D. scintillating   E. NONE MISSPELLED

8. A. arraignment   B. assassination   C. carburator   8.____
   D. irrationally   E. NONE MISSPELLED

9. A. livelihood   B. noticeable   C. optomiatic   9.____
   D. psychology   E. NONE MISSPELLED

10. A. daub   B. massacre   C. repitition   10.____
    D. requiem   E. NONE MISSPELLED

11. A. adversary   B. beneficiary   C. cemetery   11.____
    D. desultory   E. NONE MISSPELLED

12. A. criterion   B. elicit   C. incredulity   12.____
    D. omnishient   E. NONE MISSPELLED

13. A. dining   B. fiery   C. incidentally   13.____
    D. rheumatism   E. NONE MISSPELLED

14. A. collaborator   B. gaudey   C. habilitation   14.____
    D. logician   E. NONE MISSPELLED

15. A. dirge   B. ogle   C. recumbent   15.____
    D. reminiscence   E. NONE MISSPELLED

16. A. conscientious   B. renunciation   C. inconvenient   16.____
    D. inoculate   E. NONE MISSPELLED

17. A. crystalline   B. scimitar   C. ecstacy   17.____
    D. vestigial   E. NONE MISSPELLED

75

18.	A. phlegmatic D. refectory		B. rhythm E. *NONE MISSPELLED*		C. plebescite	18.____
19.	A. resilient D. sobriety		B. resevoir E. *NONE MISSPELLED*		C. recipient	19.____
20.	A. privilege D. basilisk		B. leige E. *NONE MISSPELLED*		C. leisure	20.____

KEY (CORRECT ANSWERS)

1. A. commensurable
2. B. dilapidated
3. E. None Misspelled
4. B. influential
5. E. None Misspelled
6. C. luxuriant
7. E. None Misspelled
8. C. carburetor
9. C. optimistic
10. C. repetition
11. E. None Misspelled
12. D. omniscient
13. E. None Misspelled
14. B. gaudy
15. E. None Misspelled
16. E. None Misspelled
17. C. ecstasy
18. C. plebiscite
19. B. reservoir
20. B. liege

TEST 6

DIRECTIONS: In each of the following tests in this part, select the letter of the one MIS-SPELLED word in each of the following groups of words. If no word is misspelled, select the last item, letter E (none misspelled). *PRINT THE LETTER OF THE CORRECT ANSWER IN THE SPACE AT THE RIGHT.*

1. A. repellent B. elliptical C. paralelling 1._____
   D. colossal E. *NONE MISSPELLED*

2. A. uproarious B. grievous C. armature 2._____
   D. tabular E. *NONE MISSPELLED*

3. A. ammassed B. embarrassed C. promissory 3._____
   D. asymmetrical E. *NONE MISSPELLED*

4. A. maintenance B. correspondence C. benificence 4._____
   D. miasmic E. *NONE MISSPELLED*

5. A. demurred B. occurrence C. temperament 5._____
   D. abhorrance E. *NONE MISSPELLED*

6. A. proboscis B. lucious C. mischievous 6._____
   D. vilify E. *NONE MISSPELLED*

7. A. feasable B. divisible C. permeable 7._____
   D. forcible E. *NONE MISSPELLED*

8. A. courteous B. venemous C. heterogeneous 8._____
   D. lustrous E. *NONE MISSPELLED*

9. A. millionaire B. mayonnaise C. questionaire 9._____
   D. silhouette E. *NONE MISSPELLED*

10. A. contemptible B. irreverent C. illimitable 10._____
    D. inveigled E. *NONE MISSPELLED*

11. A. prevalent B. irrelavent C. ecstasy 11._____
    D. auxiliary E. *NONE MISSPELLED*

12. A. impeccable B. raillery C. precede 12._____
    D. occurrence E. *NONE MISSPELLED*

13. A. patrolling B. vignette C. ninety 13._____
    D. surveilance E. *NONE MISSPELLED*

14. A. holocaust B. incidently C. weird 14._____
    D. canceled E. *NONE MISSPELLED*

15. A. emmendation B. gratuitous C. fissionable 15._____
    D. dilemma E. *NONE MISSPELLED*

16. A. harass B. innuendo C. capilary 16._____
    D. pachyderm E. *NONE MISSPELLED*

17. A. concomitant B. Lilliputian C. sarcophagus 17._____
    D. melifluous E. *NONE MISSPELLED*

18. A. interpolate   B. disident   C. venal
    D. inveigh   E. *NONE MISSPELLED*

19. A. supercillious   B. biennial   C. gargantuan
    D. irresistible   E. *NONE MISSPELLED*

20. A. conniving   B. expedite   C. inflammible
    D. incorruptible   E. *NONE MISSPELLED*

KEY (CORRECT ANSWERS)

1. C. paralleling
2. E. None Misspelled
3. A. amassed
4. C. beneficence
5. D. abhorrence
6. B. luscious
7. A. feasible
8. B. venomous
9. C. questionnaire
10. E. None Misspelled
11. B. irrelevant
12. E. None Misspelled
13. D. surveillance
14. B. incidentally
15. A. emendation
16. C. capillary
17. D. mellifluous
18. B. dissident
19. A. supercilious
20. C. inflammable

TEST 7

DIRECTIONS: In each of the following tests in this part, select the letter of the one MIS-SPELLED word in each of the following groups of words. If no word is misspelled, select the last item, letter E (none misspelled). *PRINT THE LETTER OF THE CORRECT ANSWER IN THE SPACE AT THE RIGHT.*

1. A. torturous B. omniscient C. hymenial 1.____
   D. flaccid E. NONE MISSPELLED

2. A. seige B. seize C. frieze 2.____
   D. grieve E. NONE MISSPELLED

3. A. indispensible B. euphony C. victuals 3.____
   D. receptacle E. NONE MISSPELLED

4. A. schism B. fortissimo C. innocuous 4.____
   D. epicurian E. NONE MISSPELLED

5. A. sustenance B. vilefy C. maintenance 5.____
   D. rarefy E. NONE MISSPELLED

6. A. desiccated B. alleviate C. beneficence 6.____
   D. preponderance E. NONE MISSPELLED

7. A. battalion B. incubus C. sacrilegious 7.____
   D. innert E. NONE MISSPELLED

8. A. shiboleth B. connoisseur C. potpourri 8.____
   D. dichotomy E. NONE MISSPELLED

9. A. pamphlet B. similar C. parlament 9.____
   D. benefited E. NONE MISSPELLED

10. A. genealogy B. tyrannical C. diletante 10.____
    D. abhorrence E. NONE MISSPELLED

11. A. effeminate B. concensus C. agglomeration 11.____
    D. fission E. NONE MISSPELLED

12. A. narcissus B. lyceum C. odissey 12.____
    D. peccadillo E. NONE MISSPELLED

13. A. stupefied B. psychiatry C. onerous 13.____
    D. frieze E. NONE MISSPELLED

14. A. intelligible B. semaphore C. pronounciation 14.____
    D. albumen E. NONE MISSPELLED

15. A. annihilate B. tyrannical C. occurence 15.____
    D. allergy E. NONE MISSPELLED

16. A. gauging B. probossis C. specimen 16.____
    D. its E. NONE MISSPELLED

17. A. diphthong B. connoisseur C. iresistible 17.____
    D. dilemma E. NONE MISSPELLED

18.	A. affect D. seize		B. baccillus E. *NONE MISSPELLED*		C. beige	18.____
19.	A. apostasy D. epigrammatic		B. sustenance E. *NONE MISSPELLED*		C. synonym	19.____
20.	A. discernable D. complement		B. consul E. *NONE MISSPELLED*		C. efflorescence	20.____

KEY (CORRECT ANSWERS)

1. C. hymeneal
2. A. siege
3. A. indispensable
4. D. epicurean
5. B. vilify
6. E. None Misspelled
7. D. inert
8. A. shibboleth
9. C. parliament
10. C. dilettante
11. B. consensus
12. C. odyssey
13. E. None Misspelled
14. C. pronunciation
15. C. occurrence
16. B. proboscis
17. C. irresistible
18. B. bacillus
19. E. None Misspelled
20. A. discernible

TEST 8

DIRECTIONS: In each of the following tests in this part, select the letter of the one MISSPELLED word in each of the following groups of words. If no word is misspelled, select the last item, letter E (none misspelled). *PRINT THE LETTER OF THE CORRECT ANSWER IN THE SPACE AT THE RIGHT.*

1. A. righteous B. seafareing C. colloquial 1.____
   D. contumely E. *NONE MISSPELLED*

2. A. sanitarium B. vicissitude C. mischievious 2.____
   D. chlorophyll E. *NONE MISSPELLED*

3. A. captain B. theirs C. asceticism 3.____
   D. acquiesced E. *NONE MISSPELLED*

4. A. across B. her's C. democracy 4.____
   D. signature E. *NONE MISSPELLED*

5. A. villain B. vacillate C. imposter 5.____
   D. temperament E. *NONE MISSPELLED*

6. A. idyllic B. volitile C. obloquy 6.____
   D. emendation E. *NONE MISSPELLED*

7. A. heinous B. sattelite C. dissident 7.____
   D. ephemeral E. *NONE MISSPELLED*

8. A. ennoble B. shellacked C. vilify 8.____
   D. indissoluble E. *NONE MISSPELLED*

9. A. argueing B. intrepid C. papyrus 9.____
   D. foulard E. *NONE MISSPELLED*

10. A. guttural B. acknowleging C. isosceles 10.____
    D. assonance E. *NONE MISSPELLED*

11. A. shoeing B. exorcise C. development 11.____
    D. irreperable E. *NONE MISSPELLED*

12. A. counseling B. cancellation C. kidnapped 12.____
    D. repellant E. *NONE MISSPELLED*

13. A. disatisfy B. misstep C. usually 13.____
    D. gregarious E. *NONE MISSPELLED*

14. A. unparalleled B. beggar C. embarrass 14.____
    D. ecstacy E. *NONE MISSPELLED*

15. A. descendant B. poliomyelitis C. privilege 15.____
    D. tragedy E. *NONE MISSPELLED*

16. A. nullify B. siderial C. salability 16.____
    D. irrelevant E. *NONE MISSPELLED*

17. A. paraphenalia B. apothecaries C. occurrence 17.____
    D. plagiarize E. *NONE MISSPELLED*

18. A. asinine   B. dissonent   C. opossum   18.____
     D. indispensable   E. *NONE MISSPELLED*

19. A. orifice   B. deferrment   C. harass   19.____
     D. accommodate   E. *NONE MISSPELLED*

20. A. changeable   B. therefor   C. incidently 20.____
     D. dissatisfy   E. *NONE MISSPELLED*

KEY (CORRECT ANSWERS)

1. B. seafaring
2. C. mischievous
3. E. None Misspelled
4. B. hers
5. C. impostor
6. B. volatile
7. B. satellite
8. E. None Misspelled
9. A. arguing
10. B. acknowledging
11. D. irreparable
12. D. repellent
13. A. dissatisfy
14. D. ecstasy
15. E. None Misspelled
16. B. sidereal
17. A. paraphernalia
18. B. dissonant
19. B. deferment
20. C. incidentally

TEST 9

DIRECTIONS: In each of the following tests in this part, select the letter of the one MISSPELLED word in each of the following groups of words. If no word is misspelled, select the last item, letter E (none misspelled). *PRINT THE LETTER OF THE CORRECT ANSWER IN THE SPACE AT THE RIGHT.*

1. A. irreparably B. lovable C. comparitively 1.____
   D. audible E. *NONE MISSPELLED*

2. A. vilify B. efflorescence C. sarcophagus 2.____
   D. sacreligious E. *NONE MISSPELLED*

3. A. picnicking B. proceedure C. hypocrisy 3.____
   D. seize E. *NONE MISSPELLED*

4. A. discomfit B. sapient C. exascerbate 4.____
   D. sarsaparilla E. *NONE MISSPELLED*

5. A. valleys B. maintainance C. abridgment 5.____
   D. reticence E. *NONE MISSPELLED*

6. A. idylic B. beneficent C. singeing 6.____
   D. asterisk E. *NONE MISSPELLED*

7. A. appropos B. violoncello C. peony 7.____
   D. mucilage E. *NONE MISSPELLED*

8. A. caterpillar B. silhouette C. rhapsody 8.____
   D. frieze E. *NONE MISSPELLED*

9. A. appendicitis B. vestigeal C. colonnade 9.____
   D. tortuous E. *NONE MISSPELLED*

10. A. omlet B. diphtheria C. highfalutin 10.____
    D. miniature E. *NONE MISSPELLED*

11. A. diorama B. sustanance C. disastrous 11.____
    D. conscious E. *NONE MISSPELLED*

12. A. inelegible B. irreplaceable C. dissatisfied 12.____
    D. procedural E. *NONE MISSPELLED*

13. A. contemptible B. sacrilegious C. proffessor 13.____
    D. privilege E. *NONE MISSPELLED*

14. A. inoculate B. diptheria C. gladioli 14.____
    D. hypocrisy E. *NONE MISSPELLED*

15. A. pessimism B. ecstasy C. furlough 15.____
    D. vulnerible E. *NONE MISSPELLED*

16. A. supersede B. moccasin C. recondite 16.____
    D. rhythmical E. *NONE MISSPELLED*

17. A. Adirondack B. Phillipines C. Czechoslovakia 17.____
    D. Cincinnati E. *NONE MISSPELLED*

18. A. weird B. impromptu C. guerrila 18.____
    D. spontaneously E. *NONE MISSPELLED*

19. A. newstand B. accidentally C. tangible 19.____
    D. reservoir E. *NONE MISSPELLED*

20. A. macaroni B. mackerel C. ukulele 20.____
    D. giutar E. *NONE MISSPELLED*

KEY (CORRECT ANSWERS)

1. C. comparatively
2. D. sacrilegious
3. B. procedure
4. C. exacerbate
5. B. maintenance
6. A. idyllic
7. A. apropos
8. E. None Misspelled
9. B. vestigial
10. A. omelet
11. B. sustenance
12. A. ineligible
13. C. professor
14. B. diphtheria
15. D. vulnerable
16. E. None Misspelled
17. B. Philippines
18. C. guerrilla
19. A. newsstand
20. D. guitar

TEST 10

DIRECTIONS: In each of the following tests in this part, select the letter of the one MIS-SPELLED word in each of the following groups of words. If no word is misspelled, select the last item, letter E (none misspelled). *PRINT THE LETTER OF THE CORRECT ANSWER IN THE SPACE AT THE RIGHT.*

1. A. rescission B. sacrament C. hypocricy 1._____
   D. salable E. *NONE MISSPELLED*

2. A. rhythm B. foreboding C. withal 2._____
   D. consciousness E. *NONE MISSPELLED*

3. A. noticeable B. drunkenness C. frolicked 3._____
   D. abcess E. *NONE MISSPELLED*

4. A. supersede B. canoeing C. exorbitant 4._____
   D. vigilance E. *NONE MISSPELLED*

5. A. idiosyncrasy B. pantomine C. isosceles 5._____
   D. wintry E. *NONE MISSPELLED*

6. A. numbskull B. indispensable C. fatiguing 6._____
   D. gluey E. *NONE MISSPELLED*

7. A. dryly B. egregious C. recommend 7._____
   D. irresistable' E. *NONE MISSPELLED*

8. A. unforgettable B. mackeral C. perseverance 8._____
   D. rococo E. *NONE MISSPELLED*

9. A. mischievous B. tyranical C. desiccate 9._____
   D. battalion E. *NONE MISSPELLED*

10. A. accede B. ninth C. abyssmal 10._____
    D. commonalty E. *NONE MISSPELLED*

11. A. resplendent B. colonnade C. harass 11._____
    D. mimicking E. *NONE MISSPELLED*

12. A. dilletante B. pusillanimous C. grievance 12._____
    D. cataclysm E. *NONE MISSPELLED*

13. A. anomaly B. connoisseur C. feasable 13._____
    D. stationery E. *NONE MISSPELLED*

14. A. ennervated B. rescission C. vacillate 14._____
    D. raucous E. *NONE MISSPELLED*

15. A. liquefy B. poniard C. truculant 15._____
    D. weird E. *NONE MISSPELLED*

16. A. existance B. lieutenant C. asinine 16._____
    D. parallelogram E. *NONE MISSPELLED*

17. A. protuberant B. nuisance C. instrumental 17._____
    D. resevoir E. *NONE MISSPELLED*

18. A. sustenance B. pedigree C. supercillious 18.____
    D. clairvoyant E. *NONE MISSPELLED*

19. A. commingle B. bizarre C. gauge 19.____
    D. priviledge E. *NONE MISSPELLED*

20. A. analagous B. irresistible C. apparel 20.____
    D. hindrance E. *NONE MISSPELLED*

KEY (CORRECT ANSWERS)

1. C. hypocrisy
2. E. None Misspelled
3. D. abscess
4. E. None Misspelled
5. B. pantomime
6. A. numskull
7. D. irresistible
8. B. mackerel
9. B. tyrannical
10. C. abysmal
11. E. None Misspelled
12. A. dilettante
13. C. feasible
14. A. enervated
15. C. truculent
16. A. existence
17. D. reservoir
18. C. supercilious
19. D. privilege
20. A. analogous

TEST 11

DIRECTIONS: In each of the following tests in this part, select the letter of the one MIS-SPELLED word in each of the following groups of words. If no word is misspelled, select the last item, letter E (none misspelled). *PRINT THE LETTER OF THE CORRECT ANSWER IN THE SPACE AT THE RIGHT.*

1. A. impute B. imparshal C. immodest 1.____
   D. imminent E. *NONE MISSPELLED*

2. A. cover B. audit C. adege 2.____
   D. adder E. *NONE MISSPELLED*

3. A. promissory B. maturity C. severally 3.____
   D. accomodation E. *NONE MISSPELLED*

4. A. superintendant B. dependence C. dependents 4.____
   D. entrance E. *NONE MISSPELLED*

5. A. managable B. navigable C. passable 5.____
   D. laughable E. *NONE MISSPELLED*

6. A. tolerance B. circumference C. insurance 6.____
   D. dominance E. *NONE MISSPELLED*

7. A. diameter B. tangent C. paralell 7.____
   D. perimeter E. *NONE MISSPELLED*

8. A. providential B. personal C. accidental 8.____
   D. diagonel E. *NONE MISSPELLED*

9. A. ballast B. ballustrade C. allotment 9.____
   D. bourgeois E. *NONE MISSPELLED*

10. A. diverse B. pedantic C. mishapen 10.____
    D. transient E. *NONE MISSPELLED*

11. A. surgeon B. sturgeon C. luncheon 11.____
    D. stancheon E. *NONE MISSPELLED*

12. A. pariah B. estrang C. conceive 12.____
    D. puncilious E. *NONE MISSPELLED*

13. A. camouflage B. serviceable C. mischievious 13.____
    D. menace E. *NONE MISSPELLED*

14. A. forefeit B. halve C. hundredth 14.____
    D. illusion E. *NONE MISSPELLED*

15. A. filial B. arras C. pantomine 15.____
    D. filament E. *NONE MISSPELLED*

16. A. llama B. madrigal C. martinet 16.____
    D. laxitive E. *NONE MISSPELLED*

17. A. symtom B. serum C. antiseptic 17.____
    D. aromatic E. *NONE MISSPELLED*

18. A. erasable   B. irascible   C. audable   18._____
    D. laudable   E. *NONE MISSPELLED*

19. A. heroes   B. folios   C. sopranos   19._____
    D. cargos   E. *NONE MISSPELLED*

20. A. latent   B. goddess   C. aisle   20._____
    D. whose   E. *NONE MISSPELLED*

KEY (CORRECT ANSWERS)

1. B. impartial
2. C. adage
3. D. accommodation
4. A. superintendent
5. A. manageable
6. E. None Misspelled
7. C. parallel
8. D. diagonal
9. B. balustrade
10. C. misshapen
11. D. stanchion
12. B. estrange
13. C. mischievous
14. A. forfeit
15. C. pantomime
16. D. laxative
17. A. symptom
18. C. audible
19. D. cargoes
20. E. None Misspelled

TEST 12

DIRECTIONS: In each of the following tests in this part, select the letter of the one MISSPELLED word in each of the following groups of words. If no word is misspelled, select the last item, letter E (none misspelled). *PRINT THE LETTER OF THE CORRECT ANSWER IN THE SPACE AT THE RIGHT.*

1. A. coconut B. bustling C. abducter 1.____
   D. naphtha E. *NONE MISSPELLED*

2. A. seriatim B. quadruped C. diphthong 2.____
   D. concensus E. *NONE MISSPELLED*

3. A. sanction B. propencity C. parabola 3.____
   D. despotic E. *NONE MISSPELLED*

4. A. circumstantial B. imbroglio C. coalesce 4.____
   D. ductill E. *NONE MISSPELLED*

5. A. spontaneous B. superlitive C. telepathy 5.____
   D. thesis E. *NONE MISSPELLED*

6. A. adobe B. apellate C. billion 6.____
   D. chiropody E. *NONE MISSPELLED*

7. A. combatant B. helium C. esprit de corps 7.____
   D. debillity E. *NONE MISSPELLED*

8. A. iota B. gopher C. demoralize 8.____
   D. culvert E. *NONE MISSPELLED*

9. A. invideous B. gourmand C. embryo 9.____
   D. despicable E. *NONE MISSPELLED*

10. A. dispeptic B. dromedary C. dormant 10.____
    D. duress E. *NONE MISSPELLED*

11. A. spiggot B. suffrage C. technology 11.____
    D. thermostat E. *NONE MISSPELLED*

12. A. aberration B. antropology C. bayou 12.____
    D. cashew E. *NONE MISSPELLED*

13. A. ricochet B. poncho C. oposum 13.____
    D. melee E. *NONE MISSPELLED*

14. A. semester B. quadrent C. penchant 14.____
    D. mustang E. *NONE MISSPELLED*

15. A. rhetoric B. polygimy C. optimum 15.____
    D. mendicant E. *NONE MISSPELLED*

16. A. labyrint B. hegira C. ergot 16.____
    D. debenture E. *NONE MISSPELLED*

17. A. solvant B. radioactive C. photostat 17.____
    D. nominative E. *NONE MISSPELLED*

18.	A. sporadic D. thorax	B. excelsior E. *NONE MISSPELLED*	C. tenible	18.____
19.	A. mischievous D. alien	B. bouillon E. *NONE MISSPELLED*	C. asinine	19.____
20.	A. sanguinery D. minutia	B. prolix E. *NONE MISSPELLED*	C. harangue	20.____

KEY (CORRECT ANSWERS)

1. C. abductor
2. D. consensus
3. B. propensity
4. D. ductile
5. B. superlative
6. B. appellate
7. D. debility
8. E. None Misspelled
9. A. invidious
10. A. dyspeptic
11. A. spigot
12. B. anthropology
13. C. opossum
14. B. quadrant
15. B. polygamy
16. A. labyrinth
17. A. solvent
18. C. tenable
19. E. None Misspelled
20. A. sanguinary

TEST 13

DIRECTIONS: In each of the following tests in this part, select the letter of the one MIS-SPELLED word in each of the following groups of words. If no word is misspelled, select the last item, letter E (none misspelled). *PRINT THE LETTER OF THE CORRECT ANSWER IN THE SPACE AT THE RIGHT.*

1. A. controvert   B. cache   C. auricle   1._____
    D. impromptu   E. *NONE MISSPELLED*

2. A. labial   B. heffer   C. intrigue   2._____
    D. decagon   E. *NONE MISSPELLED*

3. A. statistics   B. syllable   C. tenon   3._____
    D. tituler   E. *NONE MISSPELLED*

4. A. lenient   B. migraine   C. embarras   4._____
    D. nepotism   E. *NONE MISSPELLED*

5. A. lichen   B. horoscope   C. orthadox   5._____
    D. pageant   E. *NONE MISSPELLED*

6. A. libretto   B. humis   C. fallacy   6._____
    D. dextrose   E. *NONE MISSPELLED*

7. A. clinical   B. alimoney   C. bourgeois   7._____
    D. proverbial   E. *NONE MISSPELLED*

8. A. dictator   B. clipper   C. braggadoccio   8._____
    D. assuage   E. *NONE MISSPELLED*

9. A. reverence   B. hydraulic   C. felon   9._____
    D. diaphram   E. *NONE MISSPELLED*

10. A. retrobution   B. polyp   C. optician   10._____
    D. mentor   E. *NONE MISSPELLED*

11. A. resonant   B. helicopter   C. rejoicing   11._____
    D. decisive   E. *NONE MISSPELLED*

12. A. renigade   B. restitution   C. faculty   12._____
    D. devise   E. *NONE MISSPELLED*

13. A. solicitors   B. gratuitous   C. spherical   13._____
    D. crusible   E. *NONE MISSPELLED*

14. A. spongy   B. ramify   C. pica   14._____
    D. noxtious   E. *NONE MISSPELLED*

15. A. automaton   B. cadence   C. consummate   15._____
    D. ancillery   E. *NONE MISSPELLED*

16. A. magnanimous   B. iminent   C. tonsillitis   16._____
    D. dowager   E. *NONE MISSPELLED*

17. A. aerial   B. apprehend   C. bilinear   17._____
    D. transum   E. *NONE MISSPELLED*

18.	A. vacuum D. warbler	B. idiom E. *NONE MISSPELLED*	C. veriety		18.____
19.	A. zephyr D. nonpareil	B. rarify E. *NONE MISSPELLED*	C. physiology		19.____
20.	A. risque D. meridian	B. posterity E. *NONE MISSPELLED*	C. opus		20.____

KEY (CORRECT ANSWERS)

1. E. None Misspelled
2. B. heifer
3. D. titular
4. C. embarrass
5. C. orthodox
6. B. humus
7. B. alimony
8. C. braggadocio
9. D. diaphragm
10. A. retribution
11. E. None Misspelled
12. A. renegade
13. D. crucible
14. D. noxious
15. D. ancillary
16. B. imminent
17. D. transom
18. C. variety
19. B. rarefy
20. D. meridian

TEST 14

DIRECTIONS: In each of the following tests in this part, select the letter of the one MISSPELLED word in each of the following groups of words. If no word is misspelled, select the last item, letter E (none misspelled). *PRINT THE LETTER OF THE CORRECT ANSWER IN THE SPACE AT THE RIGHT.*

1. A. pygmy B. seggregation C. clayey 1.____
   D. homogeneous E. *NONE MISSPELLED*

2. A. homeopathy B. predelection C. hindrance 2.____
   D. guillotine E. *NONE MISSPELLED*

3. A. cumulative B. dandelion C. incission 3.____
   D. malpractice E. *NONE MISSPELLED*

4. A. paradise B. allegiance C. frustrate 4.____
   D. impecunious E. *NONE MISSPELLED*

5. A. licquor B. mousse C. exclamatory 5.____
   D. disciple E. *NONE MISSPELLED*

6. A. lame B. winesome C. valvular 6.____
   D. unadvised E. *NONE MISSPELLED*

7. A. Terre Haute B. Cyrano de Bergerac C. Stamboul 7.____
   D. Roosvelt E. *NONE MISSPELLED*

8. A. perambulator B. ruminate C. litturgy 8.____
   D. staple E. *NONE MISSPELLED*

9. A. hectic B. inpregnate C. otter 9.____
   D. muscat E. *NONE MISSPELLED*

10. A. lighterage B. lumbar C. insurence 10.____
    D. monsoon E. *NONE MISSPELLED*

11. A. lethal B. iliterateness C. manifold 11.____
    D. minuet E. *NONE MISSPELLED*

12. A. forfeit B. halve C. hundredth 12.____
    D. illusion E. *NONE MISSPELLED*

13. A. dissolute B. conundrum C. fallacious 13.____
    D. descrimination E. *NONE MISSPELLED*

14. A. diva B. codicile C. expedient 14.____
    D. garrison E. *NONE MISSPELLED*

15. A. filial B. arras C. pantomine 15.____
    D. filament E. *NONE MISSPELLED*

16. A. inveigle B. paraphenalia C. archivist 16.____
    D. complexion E. *NONE MISSPELLED*

17. A. dessicate B. ambidextrous C. meritorious 17.____
    D. revocable E. *NONE MISSPELLED*

18. A. queue B. isthmus C. committal 18.____
    D. binnocular E. *NONE MISSPELLED*

19. A. changeable B. abbreviating C. regretable 19.____
    D. japanned E. *NONE MISSPELLED*

20. A. Saskechewan B. Bismarck C. Albuquerque 20.____
    D. Apennines E. *NONE MISSPELLED*

KEY (CORRECT ANSWERS)

1. B. segregation
2. B. predilection
3. C. incision
4. E. None Misspelled
5. A. liquor
6. B. winsome
7. D. Roosevelt
8. C. liturgy
9. B. impregnate
10. C. insurance
11. B. illiterateness
12. E. None Misspelled
13. D. discrimination
14. B. codicil
15. C. pantomime
16. B. paraphernalia
17. A. desiccate
18. D. binocular
19. C. regrettable
20. A. Saskatchewan

TEST 15

DIRECTIONS: In each of the following tests in this part, select the letter of the one MISSPELLED word in each of the following groups of words. If no word is misspelled, select the last item, letter E (none misspelled). *PRINT THE LETTER OF THE CORRECT ANSWER IN THE SPACE AT THE RIGHT.*

1. A. culinery   B. millinery   C. humpbacked   1.____
   D. improvise   E. NONE MISSPELLED

2. A. Brittany   B. embarrassment   C. coifure   2.____
   D. leveled   E. NONE MISSPELLED

3. A. minnion   B. aborgine   C. antagonism   3.____
   D. arabesque   E. NONE MISSPELLED

4. A. tractible   B. camouflage   C. permanent   4.____
   D. dextrous   E. NONE MISSPELLED

5. A. inequitous   B. kilowatt   C. weasel   5.____
   D. lunging   E. NONE MISSPELLED

6. A. palatable   B. odious   C. motif   6.____
   D. Maltese   E. NONE MISSPELLED

7. A. Beau Brummel   B. Febuary   C. Bedouin   7.____
   D. Damascus   E. NONE MISSPELLED

8. A. llama   B. madrigal   C. illitive   8.____
   D. marlin   E. NONE MISSPELLED

9. A. babboon   B. dossier   C. esplanade   9.____
   D. frontispiece   E. NONE MISSPELLED

10. A. thrashing   B. threshing   C. atavism   10.____
    D. artifect   E. NONE MISSPELLED

11. A. ballast   B. ballustrade   C. allotment   11.____
    D. bourgeois   E. NONE MISSPELLED

12. A. amenuensis   B. saccharine   C. hippopotamus   12.____
    D. rhinoceros   E. NONE MISSPELLED

13. A. maintenance   B. bullion   C. khaki   13.____
    D. libarian   E. NONE MISSPELLED

14. A. diverse   B. pedantic   C. mishapen   14.____
    D. transient   E. NONE MISSPELLED

15. A. exhilirate   B. avaunt   C. avocado   15.____
    D. avocation   E. NONE MISSPELLED

16. A. narcotic   B. flippancy   C. daffodil   16.____
    D. narcisus   E. NONE MISSPELLED

17. A. inflamation   B. disfranchisement   C. surmise   17.____
    D. adviser   E. NONE MISSPELLED

2 (#15)

18. A. syphon   B. inquiry   C. shanghaied   18.____
    D. collapsible   E. *NONE MISSPELLED*

19. A. occassionally B. antecedence   C. reprehensible   19.____
    D. inveigh   E. *NONE MISSPELLED*

20. A. crescendos   B. indispensible   C. mosquitoes   20.____
    D. impeccable   E. *NONE MISSPELLED*

KEY (CORRECT ANSWERS)

1. A. culinary
2. C. coiffure
3. A. minion
4. A. tractable
5. A. iniquitous
6. E. None Misspelled
7. B. February
8. D. illative
9. A. baboon
10. D. artifact
11. B. balustrade
12. A. amanuensis
13. D. librarian
14. C. misshapen
15. A. exhilarate
16. D. narcissus
17. A. inflammation
18. E. None Misspelled
19. A. occasionally
20. B. indispensable

WRITTEN ENGLISH EXPRESSION
EXAMINATION SECTION
TEST 1

DIRECTIONS: In each of the sentences below, four portions are underlined and lettered. Read each sentence and decide whether any of the UNDERLINED parts contains an error in spelling, punctuation, or capitalization, or employs grammatical usage which would be inappropriate for carefully written English. If so, note the letter printed under the unacceptable form and indicate this choice in the space at the right. If all four of the underlined portions are acceptable as they stand, select the answer E. (No sentence contains more than ONE unacceptable form.)

1. The revised <u>procedure</u> was <u>quite</u> different <u>than</u> the one which <u>was</u> employed up
                A   B   C   D
to that time. <u>No error</u>
            E

1.____

2. <u>Blinded</u> by the storm that <u>surrounded</u> him, his plane <u>kept going</u> in <u>circles</u>.
   A   B   C   D
<u>No error</u>
E

2.____

3. They <u>should</u> give the book to <u>whoever</u> <u>they</u> think deserves <u>it</u>. <u>No error</u>
        A   B   C   D   E

3.____

4. The <u>government</u> will not consent to your <u>firm</u> <u>sending</u> that package as
       A   B   C
<u>second class</u> matter. <u>No error</u>
    D   E

4.____

5. She <u>would have</u> avoided all the trouble <u>that</u> followed if she <u>would have</u> waited
        A   B   C
ten minutes <u>longer</u>. <u>No error</u>
          D   E

5.____

6. <u>His</u> poetry, <u>when</u> it was carefully examined, showed <u>characteristics</u> not unlike
   A   B   C
<u>Wordsworth</u>. <u>No error</u>
    D   E

6.____

7. <u>In my opinion</u>, based upon long years of research, <u>I think</u> the plan offered by
       A   B
my opponent is <u>unsound</u>, because it is not <u>founded</u> on true facts. <u>No error</u>
                 C   D   E

7.____

8. The soldiers of <u>Washington's</u> army at Valley Forge <u>were</u> men ragged in
                   A   B
   <u>appearance</u> but <u>who were</u> noble in character. <u>No error</u>
      C   D   E

   8.____

9. Rabbits <u>have a distrust</u> of man <u>due to</u> the fact <u>that</u> they are <u>so often</u> shot.
                A   B   C   D
   <u>No error</u>
      E

   9.____

10. <u>This</u> is the man <u>who</u> I believe <u>is</u> best <u>qualified</u> for the position. <u>No error</u>
        A   B   C   D   E

    10.____

11. Her voice was <u>not only</u> good, but <u>she</u> also very clearly <u>enunciated</u>.
                     A   B   C   D
    <u>No error</u>
       E

    11.____

12. <u>Today he</u> is wearing a <u>different</u> suit <u>than</u> the <u>one</u> he wore yesterday. <u>No error</u>
         A   B   C   D   E

    12.____

13. Our work <u>is</u> to improve the club; if anybody <u>must</u> resign, let it <u>not</u> be you or <u>I</u>.
             A   B   C   D
    <u>No error</u>
       E

    13.____

14. There was so much talking <u>in back of</u> me <u>as</u> I <u>could</u> not <u>enjoy</u> the music.
                                       A   B   C   D
    <u>No error</u>
       E

    14.____

15. <u>Being that</u> he is that <u>kind of boy</u>, he cannot be blamed <u>for</u> the mistake.
          A   B   C   D
    <u>No error</u>
       E

    15.____

16. <u>The king, having read</u> the speech, <u>he</u> and the <u>queen</u> <u>departed</u>. <u>No error</u>
                  A   B   C   D   E

    16.____

17. I <u>am</u> <u>so tired</u> I <u>can't</u> <u>scarcely</u> stand. <u>No error</u>
      A   B   C   D   E

    17.____

18. We are <u>mailing bills</u> to our customers <u>in Canada</u>, and, <u>being</u> eager to
                    A   B   C
    clear our books before the new season opens, it is <u>to be hoped</u> they will
                                                                           D
    send their remittances promptly. <u>No error</u>
                                            E

    18.____

19. I reluctantly acquiesced to the proposal. No error   19.____
    A   B   C   D   E

20. It had lain out in the rain all night. No error   20.____
    A B   C   D   E

21. If he would have gone there, he would have seen a marvelous sight.   21.____
           A   B   C   D
    No error
        E

22. The climate of Asia Minor is somewhat like Utah. No error   22.____
                    A   B   C   D   E

23. If everybody did unto others as they would wish others to do unto them, this   23.____
         A   B   C   D
    world would be a paradise. No error
                                  E

24. This was the jockey whom I saw was most likely to win the race. No error   24.____
        A   B   C   D   E

25. The only food the general demanded was potatoes. No error   25.____
        A   B   C   D   E

KEY (CORRECT ANSWERS)

1.	C		11.	C
2.	A		12.	C
3.	B		13.	D
4.	B		14.	B
5.	C		15.	A
6.	D		16.	A
7.	B		17.	C
8.	D		18.	C
9.	B		19.	E
10.	E		20.	E

21. A
22. D
23. D
24. B
25. E

TEST 2

DIRECTIONS: In each of the sentences below, four portions are underlined and lettered. Read each sentence and decide whether any of the UNDERLINED parts contains an error in spelling, punctuation, or capitalization, or employs grammatical usage which would be inappropriate for carefully written English. If so, note the letter printed under the unacceptable form and indicate this choice in the space at the right. If all four of the underlined portions are acceptable as they stand, select the answer E. (No sentence contains more than ONE unacceptable form.)

1. A party <u>like</u> <u>that</u> <u>only</u> <u>comes</u> once a year. <u>No error</u>
        A   B   C   D   E

    1._____

2. <u>Our's</u> <u>is</u> <u>a</u> <u>swift moving</u> age. <u>No error</u>
    A   B C   D   E

    2._____

3. The <u>healthy</u> climate soon <u>restored</u> him <u>to</u> his <u>accustomed</u> vigor. <u>No error</u>
          A   B   C   D   E

    3._____

4. <u>They</u> needed six typists and hoped that <u>only</u> that <u>many</u> <u>would</u> apply for the
    A   B   C   D
position. <u>No error</u>
            E

    4._____

5. He <u>interviewed</u> people <u>whom</u> he thought had <u>something</u> <u>to impart</u>. <u>No error</u>
         A   B   C   D   E

    5._____

6. <u>Neither</u> of his three sisters <u>is</u> older <u>than</u> <u>he</u>. <u>No error</u>
    A   B   C D   E

    6._____

7. <u>Since</u> he is <u>that</u> <u>kind</u> of <u>a</u> boy, he cannot be expected to cooperate with us.
    A   B   C   D
<u>No error</u>
E

    7._____

8. <u>When passing</u> <u>through</u> the tunnel, the air pressure <u>affected</u> <u>our</u> years. <u>No error</u>
    A   B   C   D   E

    8._____

9. <u>The story having</u> a sad ending, <u>it</u> never <u>achieved</u> popularity <u>among</u> the
        A   B   C   D
students. <u>No error</u>
           E

    9._____

10. <u>Since</u> we are both hungry, <u>shall</u> we go <u>somewhere</u> for lunch? <u>No error</u>
     A   B   C   D   E

    10._____

11. Will you please bring this book down to the library and give it to my friend,
    A   B   C   D
    who is waiting for it? No error
                           E

12. You may have the book; I am finished with it. No error
        A   B   C   D   E

13. I don't know if I should mention it to her or not. No error
           A   B C   D   E

14. Philosophy is not a subject which has to do with philosophers and
                       A   B   C
    mathematics only. No error
                D   E

15. The thoughts of the scholar in his library are little different than the old woman
                                A   B
    who first said, "It's no use crying over spilt milk." No error
                    C   D   E

16. A complete system of philosophical ideas are implied in many simple
                A   B   C
    utterances. No error
        D   E

17. Even if one has never put them into words, his ideas compose a kind of a
         A   B   C   D
    philosophy. No error
                E

18. Perhaps it is well enough that most people do not attempt this formulation.
               A   B   C   D
    No error
    E

19. Leading their ordered lives, this confused body of ideas and feelings is
        A   B   C   D
    sufficient. No error
                E

20. Why should we insist upon them formulating it? No error
            A   B   C   D   E

21. Since it includes something of the wisdom of the ages, it is adequate for the
        A   B   C
    purposes of ordinary life. No error
        D   E

22. Therefore, I <u>have sought</u> to make a pattern <u>of mine,</u> <u>and so</u> there were, early
                  A   B   C
    moments of <u>my trying</u> to find out what were the elements with which I had to
                      D
    deal. <u>No error</u>
             E

    22.____

23. I <u>wanted</u> <u>to get</u> <u>what</u> knowledge I <u>could</u> about the general structure of the
        A   B   C   D
    universe. <u>No error</u>
               E

    23.____

24. I wanted to <u>know</u> <u>if</u> life <u>per se</u> had any meaning or <u>whether</u> I must strive to give
               A B   C   D
    it one. <u>No error</u>
             E

    24.____

25. <u>So,</u> in a <u>desultory</u> way, I <u>began</u> <u>to read</u>. <u>No error</u>
     A   B   C   D   E

    25.____

KEY (CORRECT ANSWERS)

1.	C		11.	B
2.	A		12.	C
3.	A		13.	B
4.	C		14.	D
5.	B		15.	B
6.	A		16.	B
7.	D		17.	A
8.	A		18.	C
9.	A		19.	A
10.	E		20.	D

21. E
22. C
23. C
24. B
25. E

WRITTEN ENGLISH EXPRESSION
EXAMINATION SECTION
TEST 1

DIRECTIONS: The following questions are designed to test your knowledge of grammar, sentence structure, correct usage, and punctuation. In each group there is one sentence that contains no errors. Select the letter of the CORRECT sentence. *PRINT THE LETTER OF THE CORRECT ANSWER IN THE SPACE AT THE RIGHT.*

1.   A. A low ceiling is when the atmospheric conditions make flying inadvisable.   1.____
   B. They couldn't tell who the card was from.
   C. No one but you and I are to help him.
   D. What kind of a teacher would you like to be?
   E. To him fall the duties of foster parent.

2.   A. They couldn't tell whom the cable was from.   2.____
   B. We like these better than those kind.
   C. It is a test of you more than I.
   D. The person in charge being him, there can be no change in policy.
   E. Chicago is larger than any city in Illinois.

3.   A. Do as we do for the celebration.   3.____
   B. Do either of you care to join us?
   C. A child's food requirements differ from the adult.
   D. A large family including two uncles and four grandparents live at the hotel.
   E. Due to bad weather, the game was postponed.

4.   A. If they would have done that they might have succeeded.   4.____
   B. Neither the hot days or the humid nights annoy our Southern visitor.
   C. Some people do not gain favor because they are kind of tactless.
   D. No sooner had the turning point come than a new issue arose.
   E. I wish that I was in Florida now.

5.   A. We haven't hardly enough tine.   5.____
   B. Immigration is when people come into a foreign country to live.
   C. After each side gave their version, the affair was over with.
   D. Every one of the cars were tagged by the police.
   E. He either will fail in his attempt or will seek other employment.

6.   A. They can't seem to see it when I explain the theory.   6.____
   B. It is difficult to find the genuine signature between all those submitted.
   C. She can't understand why they don't remember who to give the letter to
   D. Every man and woman in America is interested in his tax bill.
   E. Honor as well as profit are to be gained by these studies.

7. A. He arrived safe.
    B. I do not have any faith in John running for office.
    C. The musicians began to play tunefully and keeping the proper tempo indicated for the selection.
    D. Mary's maid of honor bought the kind of an outfit suitable for an afternoon wedding.
    E. If you would have studied the problem carefully you would have found the solution more quickly.

8. A. The new plant is to be electric lighted.
    B. The reason the speaker was offended was that the audience was inattentive.
    C. There appears to be conditions that govern his behavior.
    D. Either of the men are influential enough to control the situation.
    E. The gallery with all its pictures were destroyed.

9. A. If you would have listened more carefully, you would have heard your name called.
    B. Did you inquire if your brother were returning soon?
    C. We are likely to have rain before nightfall.
    D. Let's you and I plan next summer's vacation together.
    E. The man whom I thought was my friend deceived me.

10. A. There's a man and his wife waiting for the doctor since early this morning.
    B. The owner of the market with his assistants is applying the most modern principles of merchandise display.
    C. Every one of the players on both of the competing teams were awarded a gold watch.
    D. The records of the trial indicated that, even before attaining manhood, the murderer's parents were both dead.
    E. We had no sooner entered the room when the bell rang.

11. A. Why don't you start the play like I told you?
    B. I didn't find the construction of the second house much different from that of the first one I saw.
    C. "When", inquired the child, "Will we begin celebrating my birthday?"
    D. There isn't nothing left to do but not to see him anymore.
    E. There goes the last piece of cake and the last spoonful of ice cream.

12. A. The child could find neither the shoe or the stocking.
    B. The musicians began to play tunefully and keeping the proper tempo indicated for the selection.
    C. The amount of curious people who turned out for Opening Night was beyond calculation.
    D. I fully expected that the children would be at their desks and to find them ready to begin work,
    E. "Indeed," mused the poll-taker, "the winning candidate is much happier than I."

13. A. Just as you said, I find myself gaining weight. 13.____
    B. A teacher should leave the capable pupils engage in creative activities.
    C. The teacher spoke continually during the entire lesson, which, of course, was poor procedure.
    D. We saw him steal into the room, pick up the letter, and tear it's contents to shreds.
    E. It is so dark that I can't hardly see.

14. A. The new schedule of working hours and rates was satis factory to both employees and employer. 14.____
    B. Many common people feel keenly about the injustices of Power Politics.
    C. Mr. and Mrs. Burns felt that their grandchild was awfully cute when he waved good-bye.
    D. The tallest of the twins was also the most intelligent,
    E. Please come here and try and help me finish this piece of work.

15. A. My younger brother insists that he is as tall as me. 15.____
    B. Suffering from a severe headache all day, one dose of the prescribed medicine relieved me,
    C. "Please let my brothers and I help you with your packages," said Frank to Mrs. Powers.
    D. Every one of the rooms we visited had displays of pupils' work in them.
    E. Do you intend bringing most of the refreshments yourself?

16. A. The telephone linesmen, working steadily at their task during the severe storm, the telephones soon began to ring again. 16.____
    B. Meat, as well as fruits and vegetables, is considered essential to a proper diet.
    C. He looked like a real good boxer that night in the ring.
    D. The man has worked steadily for fifteen years before he decided to open his own business.
    E. The winters were hard and dreary, nothing could live without shelter.

17. A. No one can foretell when I will have another opportunity like that one again. 17.____
    B. The last group of paintings shown appear really to have captured the most modern techniques,
    C. We searched high and low, both in the attic and cellar, but were unsuccessful in locating mementos.
    D. None of the guests was able to give the rules of the game accurately.
    E. When you go to the library tomorrow, please bring this book to the librarian in the reference room.

18. A. After the debate, every one of the speakers realized that, given another chance, he could have done better. 18.____
    B. The reason given by the physician for the patient's trouble was because of his poor eating habits.
    C. The fog was so thick that the driver couldn't hardly see more than ten feet ahead.
    D. I suggest that you present the medal to who you think best.
    E. I don't approve of him going along.

19. A. A decision made by a man without much deliberation is sometimes no different than a slow one.
    B. By the time Mr. Brown's son will graduate Dental School, he will be twenty-six years of age.
    C. Who did you predict would win the election?
    D. The auctioneer had less stamps to sell this year than last year.
    E. Being that he is occupied, I shall not disturb him.

20. A. Having pranced into the arena with little grace and unsteady hoof for the jumps ahead, the driver reined his horse.
    B. Once the dog wagged it's tail, you knew it was a friendly animal.
    C. Like a great many artists, his life was a tragedy.
    D. When asked to choose corn, cabbage, or potatoes, the diner selected the latter.
    E. The record of the winning team was among the most noteworthy of the season.

21. A. The maid wasn't so small that she couldn't reach the top window for cleaning.
    B. Many people feel that powdered coffee produces a really good flavor.
    C. Would you mind me trying that coat on for size?
    D. This chair looks much different than the chair we selected in the store.
    E. I wish that he would have talked to me about the lesson before he presented it.

22. A. After trying unsuccessfully to land a job in the city, Will located in the country on a farm.
    B. On the last attempt, the pole-vaulter came nearly to getting hurt.
    C. The observance of Armistice Day throughout the world offers an opportunity to reflect on the horrors of war.
    D. Outside of the mistakes in spelling, the child's letter was a very good one.
    E. The annual income of New York is far greater than Florida.

23. A. Scissors is always dangerous for a child to handle.
    B. I assure you that I will not yield to pressure to sell my interest.
    C. Ask him if he has recall of the incident which took place at our first meeting.
    D. The manager felt like as not to order his usher-captain to surrender his uniform,
    E. Everyone on the boat said their prayers when the storm grew worse.

24. A. The mother of the bride climaxed the occasion by exclaiming, "I want my children should be happy forever."
    B. We read in the papers where the prospects for peace are improving.
    C. "Can I share the cab with you?" was frequently heard during the period of gas rationing.
    D. The man was enamored with his friend"s sister.
    E. Had the police suspected the ruse, they would have taken proper precautions.

25. A. The teacher admonished the other students neither to speak to John, nor should they annoy him.
    B. Fortunately we had been told that there was but one service station in that area.
    C. An usher seldom rises above a theatre manager.
    D. The epic, "Gone With the Wind," is supposed to have taken place during the Civil War Era.
    E. Now that she has been graduated she should be encouraged to make her own choice as to the career she is to follow.

KEY (CORRECT ANSWERS)

1.	E	11.	B
2.	A	12.	E
3.	A	13.	A
4.	D	14.	A
5.	E	15.	E
6.	D	16.	B
7.	A	17.	D
8.	B	18.	A
9.	C	19.	C
10.	B	20.	E
21.	B		
22.	C		
23.	B		
24.	E		
25.	B		

TEST 2

DIRECTIONS: The following questions are designed to test your knowledge of grammar, sentence structure, correct usage, and punctuation. In each group, there is one sentence that contains no errors. Select the letter of the CORRECT sentence. *PRINT THE LETTER OF THE CORRECT ANSWER IN THE SPACE AT THE RIGHT.*

1.
   A. Shall you be at home, let us say, on Sunday at two o'clock?
   B. We see Mr. Lewis take his car out of the garage daily, newly polished always.
   C. We have no place to keep our rubbers, only in the hall closet.
   D. Isn't it true what you told me about the best way to prepare for an examination?
   E. Mathematics is among my favorite subjects.

   1._____

2.
   A. The host thought the guests were of the hungry kinds so he prepared much food.
   B. The museum is often visited by students who are fond of early inventions, and especially patent attorneys.
   C. I rose to nominate the man who most of us felt was the most diligent worker in the group.
   D. The child was sent to the store to purchase a bottle of milk, and brought home fresh rolls, too.
   E. Hidden away in the closet, I found the long-lost purse.

   2._____

3.
   A. The garden tool was sent to be sharpened, and a new handle to be put on.
   B. At the end of her vacation, Joan came home with little money, but which systematic thrift soon overcame.
   C. We people have opportunities to show the rest of the world how real democracy functions.
   D. The guide paddled along, then fell in a reverie which he related the history of the region.
   E. No sooner had the curtain dropped when the audience shouted its approval in chorus.

   3._____

4.
   A. The data you need is to be made available shortly.
   B. The first few strokes of the brush were enough to convince me that Tom could paint much better than me.
   C. We inquired if we could see the owner of the store, after we waited for one hour.
   D. The highly-strung parent was aggravated by the slightest noise that the baby made.
   E. We should have investigated the cause of the noise by bringing the car to a halt.

   4._____

5.
   A. The police, investigating the crime, were successful in discovering only one possibly valuable clue.
   B. Due to an unexpected change in plans, the violin soloist did not perform.
   C. Besides being awarded a Bachelor's degree at college, the scientist has since received many honorary degrees.
   D. The data offered in advance of the recent Presidential election seems to have possessed elements of inaccuracy.
   E. I don't believe your the only one who has been asked to come here.

   5._____

6. A. I don't quite see that I will be able to completely finish the job in time.   6._____
    B. By my statement, I infer that you are guilty of the offense as charged.
    C. Wasn't it strange that they wouldn't let no one see the body?
    D. I hope that this is the kind of rolls you requested me to buy.
    E. The storekeeper distributed cigars as bonuses between his many customers.

7. A. He said he preferred the climate of Florida to California.   7._____
    B. Because of the excessive heat, a great amount of fruit juice was drunk by the guests.
    C. This week's dramatic presentation was neither as lively nor as entertaining as last week.
    D. The fashion expert believed that no one could develop new creations more successfully than him.
    E. A collection of Dicken's works is a "must" for every library.

8. A. There was such a large amount of books on the floor that I couldn't find a place for   8._____
       my rocking chair.
    B. Walking up the rickety stairs, the bottle slipped from his hands and smashed.
    C. The reason they granted his request was because he had a good record.
    D. Little Tommy was proud that the teacher always asked him to bring messages to the office.
    E. That kind of orange is grown only in Florida.

9. A. The new mayor is a resident of this city for thirty years.   9._____
    B. Do you mean to imply that had he not missed that shot he would have won?
    C. Next term I shall be studying French and history.
    D. I read in last night's paper where the sales tax is going to be abolished.
    E. In order to prevent breakage, she placed a sheet of paper between each of the plates when she packed them.

10. A. To have children vie against one another is psychologically unsound.   10._____
    B. Would anyone else care to discuss his baby?
    C. He was interested and aware of the problem.
    D. I sure would like to discover if he is motivating the lesson properly.
    E. The cloth was first lain on a flat surface; then it was pressed with a hot iron.

11. A. She graduated Barnard College twenty-five years ago.   11._____
    B. He studied the violin since he was seven.
    C. She is not so diligent a researcher as her classmate.
    D. He discovered that the new data corresponds with the facts disclosed by Werner.
    E. How could he enjoy the television program; the dog was barking and the baby was crying.

12. A. You have three alternatives: law, dentistry, or teaching.   12._____
    B. If I would have worked harder, I would have accomplished my purpose.
    C. He affected a rapid change of pace and his opponents were outdistanced.
    D. He looked prosperous, although he had been unemployed for a year.
    E. The engine not only furnishes power but light and heat as well.

13. A. The children shared one anothers toys and seemed quite happy.
    B. They lay in the sun for many hours, getting tanned.
    C. The reproduction arrived, and had been hung in the living room.
    D. First begin by calling the roll.
    E. Tell me where you hid it; no one shall ever find it.

14. A. Deliver these things to whomever arrives first.
    B. Everybody but she and me is going to the conference.
    C. If the number of patrons is small, we can serve them.
    D. When each of the contestants find their book, the debate may begin.
    E. Some people, farmers in particular, lament the substitution of butter by margarine.

15. A. After his illness, he stood in the country three weeks.
    B. If you wish to effect a change, submit your suggestions.
    C. It is silly to leave children play with knives.
    D. Play a trick on her by spilling water down her neck.
    E. There was such a crowd of people at the crossing we couldn't hardly get on the bus.

16. A. This is a time when all of us must show our faith and devotion to our country.
    B. Either you or I are certain to be elected president of the new club.
    C. The interpellation of the Minister of Finance forced him to explain his policies.
    D. After hoisting the anchor and removing the binnacle, the ship was ready to set sail.
    E. Please bring me a drink of cold water from the refrigerator.

17. A. Mistakes in English, when due to carelessness or haste, can easily be rectified.
    B. Mr. Jones is one of those persons who will try to keep a promise and usually does.
    C. Being very disturbed by what he had heard, Fred decided to postpone his decision.
    D. There is a telephone at the other end of the corridor which is constantly in use.
    E. In his teaching, he always kept the childrens' interests and needs in mind.

18. A. The lazy pupil, of course, will tend to write the minimum amount of words acceptable.
    B. His success as a political leader consisted mainly of his ability to utter platitudes in a firm and convincing manner.
    C. To be cognizant of current affairs, a person must not only read newspapers and magazines but also recent books by recognized authorities.
    D. Although we intended to have gone fishing, the sudden outbreak of a storm caused us to change our plans.
    E. It is the colleges that must take the responsibility for encouraging greater flexibility in the high-school curriculum.

19.
  A. "I am sorry," he said, "but John's answer was 'No'."
  B. A spirited argument followed between those who favored and opposed Marie's expulsion from the club.
  C. Whether a forward child should be humored or punished often depends upon the circumstances.
  D. Excessive alcoholism is certainly not conducive with efficient performance of one's work.
  E. Stroking his beard thoughtfully, an idea suddenly came to him.

19.____

20.
  A. "Take care, my children," he said sadly, "lest you not be deceived."
  B. Those continuous telephone calls are preventing Betty from completing her homework.
  C. They dug deep into the earth at the spot indicated on the map, but they found nothing.
  D. We petted and cozened the little girl until she finally stopped weeping.
  E. There was, in the mail, an inquiry for a house by a young couple with two or three bedrooms.

20.____

21.
  A. Please fill in the required information on the application form and return same by April 15.
  B. Tom was sitting there idly, watching the clouds scud across the sky.
  C. We started for home so that our parents would not suspect that anything out of the ordinary took place.
  D. The sudden abatement from the storm enabled the ladies to resume their journey.
  E. Each of the twelve members were agreed that the accused man was innocent.

21.____

22.
  A. The number of gifted students not continuing their education beyond secondary school present a nationwide problem.
  B. A man's animadversions against those he considers his enemies are usually reflections of his own inadequacies.
  C. The alembic of his fevered imagination produced some of the greatest romantic poetry of his era.
  D. The first case of smallpox dates back more than 3000 years and has gone unchecked until recently.
  E. He promised to go irregardless of the rain or snow.

22.____

23.
  A. The child picked up several of the coracles, which he had seen glittering in the sand, and brought them to his mother.
  B. He muttered in dejected tones – and no one contradicted him – "We have failed."
  C. A girl whom I believed to be she waved cheerily to me from a passing automobile.
  D. We discovered that she was a former resident of our own neighborhood who eloped some years ago with a milkman.
  E. It looks now like he will not be promoted after all.

23.____

24. A. Mary is the kind of a person on whom you can depend in any emergency.
     B. I am sure that either applicant can fill the job you offer competently and efficiently.
     C. Although we searched the entire room, the scissors was not to be found.
     D. Being that you are here, we can proceed with the discussion.
     E. In spite of our warning whistle, the huge ship continued to sail athwart our course.

25. A. The salaries earned by college graduates vary as much if not more than those earned by high school graduates.
     B. The apothegms that he felt to be so witty were all too often either trite or platitudinous.
     C. She read the letter carefully, took out one of the pages, and tore it into small pieces.
     D. A young man, who hopes to succeed, must be diligent in his work and alert to his opportunities.
     E. No one should plan a long journey for pleasure in these days.

KEY (CORRECT ANSWERS)

1.	A	11.	C
2.	C	12.	D
3.	C	13.	E
4.	E	14.	C
5.	A	15.	B
6.	D	16.	C
7.	B	17.	A
8.	E	18.	E
9.	B	19.	C
10.	B	20.	C

21. B
22. C
23. B
24. E
25. B

ENGLISH EXPRESSION
EXAMINATION SECTION
TEST 1

DIRECTIONS: Each question or incomplete statement is followed by several suggested answers or completions. Select the one that BEST answers the question or completes the statement. *PRINT THE LETTER OF THE CORRECT ANSWER IN THE SPACE AT THE RIGHT.*

Questions 1-9.

DIRECTIONS: The following sentences contain problems in grammar, usage diction (choice of words), and idiom. Some sentences are correct. No sentence contains more than one error. You will find that the error, if there is one, is underlined and lettered. Assume that all other elements of the sentence are correct and cannot be changed. In choosing answers, follow the requirements of standard written English. If there is an error, select the *one underlined* part that must be changed in order to make the sentence correct. If there is no error, mark E.

1. <u>In planning</u> your future, <u>one must be</u> as honest with yourself as possible, make careful
       A   B
   decisions about the best course <u>to follow to achieve</u> a particular purpose, and, above all,
                                            C
   have the courage <u>to stand by those</u> decisions. <u>No error</u>
                       D   E

1.____

2. <u>Even though</u> history does not actually repeat itself, knowledge <u>of</u> history <u>can give</u>
       A   B   C
   current problems a familiar, <u>less</u> formidable look. <u>No error</u>
                                  D   E

2.____

3. The Curies <u>had almost exhausted</u> their resources, and <u>for a time it seemed</u>
                         A   B
   <u>unlikely that they ever</u> would find the <u>solvent to their financial problems</u>. <u>No error</u>
          C   D   E

3.____

4. <u>If the rumors are</u> correct, Deane <u>will not be convicted</u>, for each of the officers
           A   B
   on the court realizes that Colson and Holdman may be <u>the real culprit and</u> that
                                                             C
   <u>their</u> testimony is not completely trustworthy. <u>No error</u>
     D   E

4.____

5. The citizens of Washington, <u>like Los Angeles</u>, prefer to commute by automobile, 5._____
                                    A
even though motor vehicles contribute <u>nearly as many</u> contaminants to the air
                                              B
<u>as do all other</u> sources <u>combined</u>. <u>No error</u>
        C   D   E

6. <u>By the time Robert Vasco completes</u> his testimony, every major executive of our 6._____
                        A
company but Ray Ashurst <u>and I</u> <u>will have been</u> <u>accused of</u> complicity in the stock
                          B   C   D
swindle. <u>No error</u>
              E

7. <u>Within six months</u> the store was operating <u>profitably and efficient</u>; shelves 7._____
        A   B
<u>were well stocked</u>, goods were selling rapidly, and the cash register
        C
<u>was ringing constantly</u>. <u>No error</u>
        D   E

8. Shakespeare's comedies have an advantage <u>over Shaw</u> <u>in that Shakespeare's</u> were 8._____
                                                A   B
<u>written primarily</u> to entertain and <u>not to</u> argue for a cause. <u>No error</u>
        C   D   E

9. Any true insomniac <u>is well aware of</u> the futility of <u>such measures as</u> drinking 9._____
                            A   B
hot milk, <u>regular hours, deep breathing</u>, counting sheep, and <u>concentrating on</u>
                  C   D
black velvet. <u>No error</u>
                  E

Questions 10-15.

DIRECTIONS: In each of the following sentences, some part of the sentence or the entire sentence is underlined. Beneath each sentence you will find five ways of phrasing the underlined part. The first of these repeats the original; the other four are different. If you think the original is better than any of the alternatives, choose answer A; otherwise choose one of the others. In choosing answers, follow the requirements of standard written English; that is, pay attention to grammar, choice of words, sentence construction, and punctuation. Choose the answer that produces the most effective sentence—clear and exact, without awkwardness or ambiguity. Do not make a choice that changes the meaning of the original sentence.

10. The tribe of warriors believed that boys and girls should be <u>reared separate, and,</u> 10._____
<u>as soon as he was weaned, the boys were taken from their mothers.</u>
   A. reared separate, and, as soon as he was weaned, the boys were taken
      from their mothers

B. reared separate, and, as soon as he was weaned, a boy was taken from his mother
C. reared separate, and, as soon as he was weaned, the boys were taken from their mothers
D. reared separately, and, as soon as a boy was weaned, they were taken from their mothers
E. reared separately, and, as soon as a boy was weaned, he was taken from his mother

11. <u>Despite Vesta being only the third largest, it is by far the brightest of the known asteroids.</u>
    A. Despite Vesta being only the third largest, it is by far the brightest of the known asteroids.
    B. Vesta, though only the third largest asteroid, is by far the brightest of the known ones.
    C. Being only the third largest, yet Vesta is by far the brightest of the known asteroids.
    D. Vesta, though only the third largest of the known asteroids, is by far the brightest.
    E. Vesta is only the third largest of the asteroids, it being, however, the brightest one.

11.____

12. As a result of the discovery of the Dead Sea Scrolls, our understanding of the roots of Christianity <u>has had to be revised considerably.</u>
    A. has had to be revised considerably
    B. have had to be revised considerably
    C. has had to undergo revision to a considerable degree
    D. have had to be subjected to considerable revision
    E. has had to be revised in a considerable way

12.____

13. Because <u>it is imminently suitable to</u> dry climates, adobe has been a traditional building material throughout the southwestern states.
    A. it is imminently suitable to
    B. it is eminently suitable for
    C. It is eminently suitable when in
    D. of its eminent suitability with
    E. of being imminently suitable in

13.____

14. <u>Martell is more concerned with demonstrating that racial prejudice exists than preventing it from doing harm, which explains</u> why his work is not always highly regarded.
    A. Martell is more concerned with demonstrating that racial prejudice exists than preventing it from doing harm, which explains
    B. Martell is more concerned with demonstrating that racial prejudice exists than with preventing it from doing harm, and this explains
    C. Martell is more concerned with demonstrating that racial prejudice exists than with preventing it from doing harm, an explanation of
    D. Martell's greater concern for demonstrating that racial prejudice exists than preventing it from doing harm—this explains
    E. Martell's greater concern for demonstrating that racial prejudice exists than for preventing it from doing harm explains

14.____

15. <u>Throughout this history of the American West there runs a steady commentary on the deception and mistreatment of the Indians.</u>
    A. Throughout this history of the American West there runs a steady commentary on the deception and mistreatment of the Indians.
    B. There is a steady commentary provided on the deception and mistreatment of the Indians and it runs throughout this history of the American West.
    C. The deception and mistreatment of the Indians provide a steady comment that runs throughout this history of the American West.
    D. Comment on the deception and mistreatment of the Indians is steadily provided and runs throughout this history of the American West.
    E. Running throughout this history of the American West is a steady commentary that is provided on the deception and mistreatment of the Indians.

Questions 16-20.

DIRECTIONS: In each of the following questions you are given a complete sentence to be rephrased according to the directions which follow it. You should rephrase the sentence mentally to save time, although you may make notes in your test book if you wish. Below each sentence and its directions are listed words or phrases that may occur in your revised sentence. When you have thought out a good sentence, look in the choices A through E for the word or entire phrase that is included in your revised sentence, and print the letter of the correct answer in the space at the right. The word or phrase you choose should be the most accurate and most nearly complete of all the choices given, and should be part of a sentence that meets the requirements of standard written English. Of course, a number of different sentences can be obtained if the sentence is revised according to directions, and not all of these possibilities can be included in only five choices. If you should find that you have thought of a sentence that contains none of the words or phrases listed in the choices, you should attempt to rephrase the sentence again so that it includes a word or phrase that is listed. Although the directions may at times require you to change the relationship between parts of the sentence or to make slight changes in meaning in other ways, <u>make only those changes that the directions require</u>; that is, keep the meaning the same, or as nearly the same as the directions permit. If you think that more than one good sentence can be made according to the directions, select the sentence that is most exact, effective, and natural in phrasing and construction.

EXAMPLES

I. <u>Sentence</u>: Coming to the city as a young man, he found a job as a newspaper reporter.
   <u>Directions</u>: Substitute <u>He came</u> for <u>Coming</u>.
   A. and so he found
   B. and found
   C. and there he had found
   D. and then finding
   E. and had found

5 (#1)

Your rephrased sentence will probably read: "He came to the city as a young man and found a job as a newspaper reporter." This sentence contains the correct answer: <u>B. and found</u>. A sentence which used one of the alternate phrases would <u>change the</u> meaning or <u>intention</u> of the original sentence, would be a <u>poorly written sentence</u>, or would be <u>less effective</u> than another possible revision.

II. <u>Sentence</u>: Owing to her wealth, Sarah had many suitors.
<u>Directions</u>: Begin with <u>Many men courted</u>.
   A. so   B. while   C. although   D. because   E. and

Your rephrased sentence will probably read: "Many men courted Sarah because she was wealthy." This new sentence contains only choice D, which is the correct answer. None of the other choices will fit into an effective, correct sentence that retains the original meaning.

16. The archaeologists could only mark out the burial site, for then winter came.
Begin with <u>Winter came before</u>.
   A. could do nothing more   B. could not do anything
   C. could only do   D. could do something
   E. could do anything more

16.____

17. The white reader often receives some insight into the reasons why black men are angry from descriptions by a black writer of the injustice they encounter in a white society.
Begin with <u>A black writer often gives</u>.
   A. when describing   B. by describing
   C. he has described   D. in the descriptions
   E. because of describing

17.____

18. The agreement between the university officials and the dissident students provides for student representation on every university committee and on the board of trustees.
Substitute <u>provides that</u> for <u>provides for</u>.
   A. be   B. are   C. would have
   D. would be   E. is to be

18.____

19. English Romanticism had its roots in German idealist philosophy, first described in England by Samuel Coleridge.
Begin with <u>Samuel Coleridge was the first in</u>.
   A. in which English   B. and from it English
   C. where English   D. the source of English
   E. the birth of English

19.____

20. Four months have passed since his dismissal, during which time Alan has looked for work daily.
Begin with <u>Each day</u>.
   A. will have passed   B. that have passed   C. that passed
   D. were to pass   E. had passed

20.____

KEY (CORRECT ANSWERS)

1.	B	11.	D
2.	E	12.	A
3.	D	13.	B
4.	C	14.	E
5.	A	15.	A
6.	B	16.	E
7.	B	17.	B
8.	A	18.	A
9.	C	19.	D
10.	E	20.	B

EXAMINATION SECTION
TEST 1

DIRECTIONS: Each question or incomplete statement is followed by several suggested answers or completions. Select the one that BEST answers the question or completes the statement. *PRINT THE LETTER OF THE CORRECT ANSWER IN THE SPACE AT THE RIGHT.*

Questions 1-10.

DIRECTIONS: Some of the following groups of words make correct, complete sentences. Others contain errors or are not complete sentences. If the group of words makes a correct, complete sentence, indicate 0 (ZERO). If the group of words does not make a correct, complete sentence, indicate the letter of the part which contains the error or which should be changed to make a complete sentence.

1. A. No one
   B. knows
   C. why he came
   D. or where he went.

2. A. What do you
   B. think
   C. is the answer
   D. to the problem?

3. A. What
   B. fun to be
   C. on the
   D. relay team!

4. A. Hope
   B. to win
   C. the next set
   D. of races.

5. A. The class giving
   B. a play
   C. for parents
   D. and friends

6. A. How
   B. exciting
   C. winning
   D. would be!

121

7. A. Richard
    B. likes
    C. swimming and to water ski
    D. in the summer.   7._____

8. Charles   8._____
    A. has played
    B. football for
    C. three years and
    D. will again next year.

9. He likes   9._____
    A. all sports the coach
    B. says Charles is the best
    C. all-round athlete
    D. the school has ever had.

10. A. Although the weather   10._____
    B. is cold,
    C. we can see
    D. signs of nature's reawakening

Questions 11-25.

DIRECTIONS: In each sentence below, one or more letters are underlined. Indicate C (CORRECT) or W (WRONG) in the space at the right of each sentence in which the letter or letters underlined are CORRECTLY capitalized.

11. Tom learned much about the sea from <u>c</u>aptain Jones.   11._____

12. Dear <u>s</u>ir: 12._____

13. Will you please send us information about tours through the <u>e</u>ast? I am   13._____
    especially interested in seeing

14. <u>i</u>ndia and the   14._____

15. <u>T</u>aj <u>M</u>ahal.   15._____

16. Yours <u>v</u>ery <u>s</u>incerely, John Brown   16._____

17. Jeffrey calls his dog <u>F</u>risker.   17._____

18. He bought the dog from a neighbor who lives a black <u>n</u>orth of Jeffrey. 18._____

19. He got the dog last <u>S</u>ummer.   19._____

20. Once we visited the United States <u>s</u>enate.   20._____

3 (#1)

21. Washington Irving wrote "The legend of Sleepy Hollow." 21.____
22. My uncle says that story is one of his favorites. 22.____
23. I shall always remember my drive through the Cumberland Mountains. 23.____
24. "It is early," the guide said, "but we shall be ready to start the tour soon." 24.____
25. "I am glad," Jane replied. "we are very eager to go." 25.____

Questions 26-50.

DIRECTIONS: From the list of choices below, select the punctuation mark which should be used where the parenthesis appear in each sentence. Indicate the letter of the correct answer in the space at the right.

- A. Colon
- B. Comma
- C. Dash
- D. Double quotation marks
- E. Exclamation point
- F. Hyphen
- G. Question mark
- H. Period
- I. Semicolon
- J. Single quotation marks
- K. No punctuation

26. Last night we heard a bird call from the woods near our home(). 26.____
27. We wondered what it could be() 27.____
28. Because we had not heard the call before() we did not recognize it as the song of a whippoorwill. 28.____
29. Are you ready for school now() Nancy? 29.____
30. School does not begin until 8()30. 30.____
31. I want to arrive in time to see Miss Smith() the music teacher. 31.____
32. I should like to join the chorus() but tryouts come during the time when I have band practice. 32.____
33. It is possible() of course() that band practice will be over before the tryouts are. 33.____
34. The snow() covered bushes looked like ghosts huddled together. 34.____
35. On the farm were the following() 35.____
36. cows() pigs() chickens() and geese. 36.____

123

4 (#1)

37. The farm is near Lincoln() Nebraska.   37._____

38. On our vacation, we traveled in Minnesota() and Wisconsin() and Michigan.   38._____

39. What interesting experiences we had()   39._____

40. Someone said the world would end on August 7() 1987.   40._____

41. Sammy's bright() happy smile made him popular with everyone.   41._____

42. We appreciate your help; however() it is too late to continue.   42._____

43. Da Vinci() who was famous as a painter() was also a scientist and an   43._____
    inventor.

44. Please mail the package to 412 Park Avenue() Denver.   44._____

45. Mother said the border was three and three() fourths inches wide.   45._____

46. Miss Swanson() our home economics teacher() has taught us to bake bread.   46._____

47. The Home Economics Club is for everyone() who enjoys cooking or sewing.   47._____

48. The path was steep and rough() nevertheless, we did not turn back.   48._____

49. "Father likes to quote the lines, ()He prayeth best who loveth best,()" said 49._____
    Joanne.

50. "Do you like poetry()" asked James.   50._____

KEY (CORRECT ANSWERS)

1.	O	11.	W	21.	W	31.	B	41.	B
2.	O	12.	W	22.	C	32.	B	42.	B
3.	B	13.	W	23.	C	33.	B	43.	B
4.	A	14.	W	24.	C	34.	F	44.	B
5.	A	15.	C	25.	W	35.	A	45.	F
6.	O	16.	C	26.	H	36.	B	46.	B
7.	C	17.	C	27.	H	37.	B	47.	K
8.	D	18.	C	28.	B	38.	K	48.	I
9.	A	19.	W	29.	B	39.	E	49.	J
10.	O	20.	W	30.	A	40.	B	50.	G

TEST 2

DIRECTIONS: Each question or incomplete statement is followed by several suggested answers or completions. Select the one that BEST answers the question or completes the statement. *PRINT THE LETTER OF THE CORRECT ANSWER IN THE SPACE AT THE RIGHT.*

Questions 1-10.

DIRECTIONS: In answering Questions 1 through 10, indicate the CORRECT answer.

1. Perhaps the jewelry is
   A. hers
   B. her's
   C. hers'

2. _____ the best musician in our group.
   A. You're
   B. Your

3. _____ painting did you think was most pleasing?
   A. Who's
   B. Whose

4. The children gave _____ pennies to buy a gift for the sick child.
   A. there
   B. their
   C. they're

5. It is _____ too warm for ice fishing.
   A. all together
   B. altogether

6. _____ going to rain soon.
   A. Its
   B. It's

7. The speaker used so many _____ that we found it tiresome to listen to him.
   A. wells
   B. wells'
   C. well's

8. _____ eyes were sparkling happily.
   A. Agneses
   B. Agne's
   C. Agnes's

9. We faced the mountain and called, but only our _____ answered us.
   A. echos
   B. echoes

10. Alice likes skiing and skating, _____.
    A. to
    B. two
    C. too

Questions 11-25.

DIRECTIONS: In answering Questions 11 through 25, indicate which choice makes the sentence CORRECT?

11. Paul _____ hardly started to wade when his foot slipped, and he fell into the water.
    A. had
    B. had not

12. _____ across a chair was a beautiful Spanish shawl.

13. The book had been _____ by some careless child.
    A. teared   B. tore   C. torn

14. The clown _____ a tattered hat.
    A. weared   B. wore   C. worn

15. Someone had _____ all of the orange juice.
    A. drinked   B. drank   C. drunk

16. Our dog _____ like music.
    A. don't   B. doesn't

17. The child had _____ so softly that we were not sure that we had heard him correctly.
    A. speaked   B. spoke   C. spoken

18. Jim had _____ across the pool twice before I even got started.
    A. swimmed   B. swam   C. swum

19. The _____ milk
    A. freezed   B. frozen   C. froze

20. _____ the bottle.
    A. busted   B. bursted   C. burst

21. _____ are always teasing each other.
    A. She and Joanne   B. Her and Joanne

22. Where had you _____ the drawings?
    A. lay   B. laid   C. lain

23. Children were _____ on the stairway.
    A. sitting   B. setting

24. I have _____ most of the invitations.
    A. writed   B. wrote   C. written

25. Holding onto a flimsy thread of its web,
    A. a spider swayed back and forth.
    B. we saw a spider swaying back and forth.

Questions 26-50.

DIRECTIONS: In answering Questions 26 through 50, indicate from the even-numbered items that which makes the sentence correct. Select from the odd-numbered choices that rule which makes the sentence incorrect.

3 (#2)

26. John is wittier than
    A. I B. me C. myself

27. A. Nominative case, predicate pronoun
    B. Objective case, object of a preposition
    C. Reflexive pronoun, to refer to the speaker
    D. Nominative case, subject of a verb understood

28. No one could catch Jack and
    A. I B. me C. myself

29. A. Nominative case, predicate pronoun
    B. Objective case, object of a verb
    C. Objective case, object of a preposition
    D. Reflexive pronoun, to refer to the speaker

30. One of the children _____ an excellent violinist.
    A. is B. are

31. A. Singular verb, to agree with One
    B. Singular verb, to agree with violinist
    C. Plural verb, to agree with children

32. Neither Tom nor his brothers _____ able to play yesterday.
    A. was B. were

33. A. Singular verb, to agree with Tom
    B. Singular verb, to agree with Neither
    C. Plural verb, to agree with brothers
    D. Plural verb, to agree with a compound subject

34. Either the team members or the coach _____ asked to pick up the trophy.
    A. was B. were

35. A. Singular verb, to agree with coach
    B. Singular verb, to agree with team
    C. Plural verb, to agree with members
    D. Plural verb, to agree with a compound object

36. Both of the boys _____ excellent students.
    A. is B. are

37. A. Singular verb, to agree with Both
    B. Plural verb, to agree with Both
    C. Plural verb, to agree with boys

38. Everybody at the party _____ having a good time.
    A. was B. were

39. A. Singular verb, to agree with Everybody
     B. Singular verb, too agree with party
     C. Singular verb, to agree with time
     D. Plural verb, to agree with Everybody

40. Which of the two dresses do you think is the
     A. prettier   B. prettiest

41. A. Comparative degree of an adjective
     B. Superlative degree of an adjective
     C. Comparative degree of the adverb

42. Miss Brown sent Bob and _____ postcards from France.
     A. I   B. me   C. myself

43. A. Nominative case, predicate pronoun
     B. Objective case, direct object of the verb
     C. Objective case, indirect object of the verb
     D. Reflexive pronoun, to refer to the speaker

44. Because the gift came from Jerry and _____, we appreciated it very much.
     A. he   B. him

45. A. Nominative case, predicate pronoun
     B. Objective case, object of the verb
     C. Objective case, object of a preposition

46. Everyone present had _____ own opinion about the problem.
     A. his   B. their

47. A. Singular pronoun, to refer to Everyone
     B. Singular pronoun, to refer to problem
     C. Plural pronoun, to refer to Everyone

48. It is _____ too late to call now.
     A. sure   B. surely

49. A. Adjective, to modify It
     B. Adverb, to modify is
     C. Adverb, to modify to call

50. The sunset was _____ beautiful.
     A. real   B. very

51. A. Adjective, to modify sunset
     B. Adverb, to modify was
     C. Adverb, to modify beautiful

KEY (CORRECT ANSWERS)

1. A	11. A	21. A	31. A	41. A
2. A	12. A	22. B	32. B	42. B
3. B	13. C	23. A	33. C	43. B
4. B	14. B	24. C	34. A	44. B
5. B	15. C	25. A	35. A	45. C
6. B	16. B	26. A	36. B	46. A
7. A	17. C	27. A	37. B	47. A
8. C	18. C	28. B	38. A	48. B
9. B	19. B	29. B	39. A	49. B
10. C	20. C	30. A	40. A	50. B
				51. C

TEST 3

DIRECTIONS: Each question or incomplete statement is followed by several suggested answers or completions. Select the one that BEST answers the question or completes the statement. *PRINT THE LETTER OF THE CORRECT ANSWER IN THE SPACE AT THE RIGHT.*

Questions 1-14.

DIRECTIONS: In answering Questions 1 through 14, indicate from the even-numbered items that which makes the sentence correct. Select from the odd-numbered choices that rule which makes the sentence incorrect.

1. Velvet feels
   A. soft
   B. softly

2. A. Adjective, to modify Velvet
   B. Adverb, to modify feels
   C. Adjective, to modify feels

3. Jane asked _____ rang the doorbell.
   A. who
   B. whom

4. A. Objective case, object of asked
   B. Objective case, object of rang
   C. Nominative case, subject of rang

5. For _____ did you ask when you telephoned the office?
   A. who
   B. whom

6. A. Nominative case, subject of did ask
   B. Objective case, object of the verb
   C. Objective case, object of a preposition

7. _____ can laugh at himself will probably make an agreeable companion.
   A. Whoever
   B. whomever

8. A. Nominative case, subject of will make
   B. Nominative case, subject of can laugh
   C. Objective case, object of can laugh
   D. Objective case, object of will make

9. Father thinks that _____ tries can succeed.
   A. whoever
   B. whomever

10. A. Nominative case, subject of can succeed
    B. Nominative case, subject of tries
    C. Objective case, object of thinks

11. Our government is run by _____ the people elect.   11._____
    A. whoever   B. whomever

12. A. Objective case, object of a preposition   12._____
    B. Objective case, object of elect
    C. Nominative case, predicate nominative

13. The child speaks   13._____
    A. distinct   B. distinctly

14. A. Adverb, to modify speaks   14._____
    B. Adjective, to modify child
    C. Adjective, to modify speaks

Questions 15-24.

DIRECTIONS: Indicate the letter of the part of speech which correctly describes the use of the word, phrase, or clause in the following sentences. Choose the parts of speech from the column at the right.

<u>Parts of Speech</u>

15.	Early	A. Adjective	15._____
16.	May	B. Adverb	16._____
17.	Plains	C. Conjunction	17._____
18.	was rising	D. Interjection	18._____
19.	of rosy splendor	E. Noun	19._____
20.	above	F. Preposition	20._____
21.	to be alive and free	G. Pronoun	21._____
22.	and	H. Verb	22._____
23.	the		23._____
24.	we		24._____

Questions 25-34.

DIRECTIONS: Indicate the title of the book which would be alphabetized FIRST among the choices that follow.

25. A. WIND IN THE PINES   B. NIGHT WIND   25.____
    C. IVANHOE   D. KIDNAPED

26. A. VELVET SHOES   B. USES OF COAL   26.____
    C. WONDERLAND   D. YOUNG HEROES

27. A. BUFFALO BILL   B. CARAVAN   27.____
    C. DAYS TO REMEMBER   D. FROM DAWN TO DUSK

28. A. TELEPHONE TALES   B. TELEGRAPHIC CODES   28.____
    C. TEMPEST IN A TEAPOT   D. TELLING SEA TALES

29. A. LEARNING TO SWIM   29.____
    B. THE LAST LEAF
    C. THE SPIDER
    D. THE MAN WITHOUT A COUNTRY

30. A. FOG   B. THE GYPSY   30.____
    C. HOBBIES   D. A PECK OF GOLD

31. A. SKATING   B. SILVER SHIPS   31.____
    C. THE MAN WITH THE MASK D. TIMBER COUNTRY

32. A. WILD ANIMALS I HAVE KNOWN   32.____
    B. FOOL'S GOLD
    C. THE JESTER
    D. UNCLE JAKE'S ADVENTURES WITH A WILDCAT

33. A. PAUL REVERE'S RIDE   B. PRIVATE ZOO   33.____
    C. LOCHINVAR   D. TOP SECRET

34. A. ONCE UPON A STORYTIME   34.____
    B. HEROES OF PROGRESS
    C. HEART, HEALTH, AND HAPPINESS
    D. HENRIETTA HARVEY'S HAVEN

KEY (CORRECT ANSWERS)

1. A	11. B	21. F	31. C
2. A	12. A	22. C	32. B
3. A	13. B	23. A	33. C
4. C	14. A	24. G	34. C
5. B	15. A	25. C	
6. C	16. E	26. B	
7. A	17. E	27. A	
8. B	18. H	28. B	
9. A	19. F	29. B	
10. A	20. A	30. A	

PRINCIPLES AND PRACTICES OF TRANSCRIPTION

TABLE OF CONTENTS

		Page
I.	30 RULES FOR CORRECT TRANSCRIPTION	1
II.	LIST OF DIVISION DEMONS IN TRANSCRIPTION (WITH ACCENT MARKS)	3
	Abate................ Axiomatic	3
	Bacteria............ Demonstrative	4
	Deodorant .... Itinerary	5
	Jovial .... yeoma	6
	Strenuous......... Zoology	7

PRINCIPLES AND PRACTICES OF TRANSCRIPTION

I. 30 RULES FOR CORRECT TRANSCRIPTION

   1. *CORRECT:* Type date on one line
      INCORRECT: Break the date up, as: May 15,1968

   2. *CORRECT:* Type Mr. James Doe on one line.
      INCORRECT: Break it up, as: Mr. James Doe

   3. *CORRECT:* Type address together.
      INCORRECT: Break the address up, as: 42 Sixth Avenue.

   4. *CORRECT:* Divide a word so that more than one letter is on a line.
      INCORRECT: Divide the word so that only one letter is on a line, as: a-lone.

   5. *CORRECT:* Divide a word so that more than two letters are on the following line.
      INCORRECT: Divide a word so that two letters remain on the second line, as remind-ed.

   6. Both enclosed and inclosed are'correct. Make sure that Enc. or Inc. under the initials match the word in the letter.

   7. *CORRECT:* Copy the address from a letter or information sheet correctly. For instance, if Mr. Elliott Davis is in the letter or sheet (two 1's), copy it exactly.
      INCORRECT: Type Eliott with one 1.

   8. Type My dear Sir:-- dear with a small d.

   9. Use a number for the date when the month is typed first, as May 3. Otherwise, write the number in word form: for example, the third of May.

   10. Leave off st, nd, rd, th, from the number if the month is typed first; for example, May 1, May 2, May 3, May 4.

   11. A medium-sized letter should have at least two paragraphs. Sometimes a short note or letter will have only one paragraph. Indicate a new paragraph when the thought changes.

   12. Type the dictator's initials and your initials four single spaces below the complimentary closing. Enc. or Inc. is typed directly below the initials.

   13. *CORRECT:* ype Fifth Avenue, rather than 5th Avenue.
       INCORRECT: Write 5th in your shorthand notes as the letters that would be considered longhand. The $ sign and % sign are considered longhand, too.

14. *CORRECT:* Use the MR key when erasing.
    INCORRECT: Erase over the key basket.

15. Clean up your letter before handing it in. Erase smudge marks and other marks which detract from the attractiveness of your work.

16. Check each letter before removing it from the machine. Check word for word with your stenography notes.

17. *CORRECT:* Use your dictionary if you are not sure of a spelling or word division.
    INCORRECT: Guess at spelling or word division.

18. Don't overpunctuate. "When in doubt, leave it out" is a good rule to follow. Too many commas are wrong - and in poor taste.

19. When expressions such as: of course, no doubt, therefore, however, etc., occur in the middle of a sentence, use commas before and after. One comma is incorrect. If a sentence should begin with these words, always put a comma immediately after the expression, as: Therefore, we ask that you call us as soon as you can.

20. Whenever a sentence ends, space twice before starting the next sentence. However, after a semi-colon, comma, or abbreviation (Mr.) leave one space.

21. Words or phrases in a series are separated by commas, as: The colors of our flag are red, white, and blue.

22. After an introductory clause, use a comma, as: Since you were here, many things have changed.

23. When two independent clauses are joined by <u>and</u>, <u>but</u>, <u>or</u>,--use a comma after the first clause, as: I expect to see you, and I hope you will be on time.

24. Words starting with <u>over</u> or <u>under</u> are spelled as one word, as overpaid, overdue, oversight, overwork, underpaid, undersell, undertones.

25. When two or more words are used as a single adjective to describe a noun following immediately, hyphenate, as: up-to-date home, first-class mail, low-priced articles. However, if the noun does not follow immediately, omit the hyphen, as: a home that is up to date.

26. If several adjectives are used to describe one noun, treat as you would words in a series, as: a warm, red coat.

27. Don't divide a word that already has a hyphen, as: self-control.

28. <u>Passed</u> is a verb. When we refer to a bill that is <u>past</u> due, we are referring to a matter of time.

29. Eliminate "flying" capitals by holding your shift key down a trifle longer.

30. When you are comparing something, use <u>than</u>. <u>Then</u> refers to time. 'For example: more than, better than, prettier than, smaller than.
Get your mother's permission, and <u>then</u> we can go on a trip. She pays less rent <u>than</u> you.

II. LIST OF DIVISION DEMONS IN TRANSCRIPTION (WITH ACCENT MARKS)

a bate'	ag' ri cul ture	a' pri cot
ata do' men	a larm'	ar' bi trar y
a bom' i na ble	a' li as	ar cade'
ab' ro gate	al' ien ate	ar' chi tec ture
ab sen tee'	al' i mon y	ar' du ous
ab' so lute ly	al lies'	a' ri a
ab sorb'	al read' y	a ris' to crat
ab' sti nence	am a teur'	ar ma' da
ab surd'	am bi gu' i ty	ar' ro gance
ac a dem' ic	a men' i ty	a skance'
ac eel' er ate	A mer' i can	a skew'
ac ces' so ry	a' mi a ble	as pir' ant
ac cli' mate	am ne' si a	as' ter isk
ac com' pa nist	an' arch y	ath' lete
a cu' men	an ces' tral	ath let' ics
ad' a mant	an' ec dote	a torn' ic
ad dress'	an ni' hi late	au da' cious
a dept'	an nu' i ty	au di to' ri urn
ad' mi ra ble	an tag' o nist	au gust'
ad o les' cent	an te ced' ent	aunt
ad vance'	an tic' i pate	a vi a' tion
ad' ver sar y	ap a thet' ic	a' vi a tor
ad ver' tise ment	ap pa ra' tus	ax i o mat' i c
af fi da' vit	ap par' ent	
a' gen cy	ap' pli ca ble	
ag gres' sor	ap pro ba' tion	

bac te' ri a
bade
bal' let
bal' lot
ban' quet
bap' tism
bar' ba rous
be cause'
bel lig' er ent
ben e fi' ci ar y
be nev' o lent
be troth' al
be yond'
bi' as
bi en' ni al
big' a my
big' ot ry
bi og' ra phy
bi tu' mi nous
bi zarre'
black' guard
blas' phe my
bludg' oen
bo le' ro
bou' doir
bour geois'
bra va' do
brig' and
bron' chi al
bru nette'
buc ca neer'
bu reauc' ra cy

cab' a ret
caf e te' ri a
can' o py

ca price'
car' a mel
car' a van
car' i ca ture
car' ni val
cas' se role
ca tas' tro phe
cat' e go ry
cav i ar'
ce leb' ri ty
ce ment'
cen trif' u gal
cha grin'
cha let'
cham' ois
cham' pi on
cha ot' ic
chasm
chas' tise ment
chauf feur'
chi can' er y
chiv' al ric
chrys an' the mum
cig a rette'
clan des' tine
clean' li ness
clem' en cy
cli che'
cli en tele'
clique
co a li' tion
coif fure'
col lo' qui al
colo' nel
co los' sal
com' bat ant

com' fort a ble
com mu ni que'
com' pa ra ble
com' pe tent
com pla' cent
con cer' to
con coct'
con do' lence
con gen' ial
con nois seur'
con ta' gious
con tern' po rar y
con tin' u ous
con' tro ver sy
con' ver sant
co quette'
cor' o net
cor' pu lent
cos turn' er
cou' pon
cov' et ous
cred' u lous
cri te' ri on
cu' bi cle
cu' li nar y
deaf
de bate'
de but'
dec' ade
de dine'
dec' o rous
de co' rum
def' i cit
del i ca tes' sen
de lin' quent
de mon' stra tive

de o' dor ant
de plor' a ble
de pos' i tor
de' pot
dep ri va' tion
der' e lict
des' pi ca ble
det' ri ment
di' a mond
di' a per
die ta' tor
di gress'
di late'
di lem' ma
di' o cese
di plo' ma
di plo' ma cy
dir' i gi ble
dis as' ter
dis cern'
dis cre' tion
di shev' el
dis in' ter est ed
dis par' age
dis' pu ta ble
dis' si pate
dis tin' guish
di vulge'
doc' ile
dog' ged
dog' ma
dom' i cile
du' bi ous

ec cen' trie
e con' o my
ec' sta sy
e' diet
ef feet'
e' go tist
e lee' toral
em' a nate
em ploy ee'
en cy clo pe' di a
en' er gy
en' ter prise
en tire'
en vel' opv-(y.)
en' ve lope (n .)
en vi' ron ment

ep' i cure
e qua to' ri al
eg' ui ta ble
eq' ui ty
er ro' ne ous
es' pi o nage
eth' ics
et' i quette
eu' lo gy
eu' phe mism
ev' i dent ly
ex as' per ated
ex cise'
ex' i gen cies
ex' o dus
ex og' a my
ex ot' ic
ex pe' di ent
ex pense'
ex per' i ment
ex' qui site
ex tra' ne ous
ex' tri cate
fac sim' i le
fau' cet
Feb' ru ar y
fi as' co
fie ti' tious
fig' ur a tive
fil' i bus ter film
fi na' le
fin an cier'
fi nesse'
for bade'
fore' head
fore' most
for' mi da ble
frag' ile
frag' men tar y
frus tra' tion
fu' tile
ga' la
gal' ax y
ga rage'
gen' u ine
gi gan' tic
gov' ern ment

griev' ous
gri mace'
guar an tee'
hab' i tat
hang' ar
haz' ard ous
hearth
her' e sy
he ro' ic
hes' i tan cy
hi lar' i ous
hon' or a ble
ho ri' zon
ho tel'
hu' man
hu mane'
hy poc' ri sy
hys ter' i cal
id' i om
ig' no min y
ig no ra' mus
il lit' er ate
im pet' u ous
im' pi ous
im pla' ca ble
im pos' tor
im' po tent
im promp' tu
im' pro vise
in ap' pli ca ble
in clem' ent
in. con' gru ous
in diet' ment
in' do lent
in er' tia
in fal' li ble
in' flu ence
in quir' y
in sane'
in' ter est
in vei' gle
in' ven to ry
i ' o dine
i ' rate
ir ref' u ta ble
ir rev' o ca ble
i ' so late
i tin' er ar y

jo' vi al
ju di' cial
ju' ve nile
ker' o sene
ki mo' no
lam' en ta ble
lan' guage
leg' end
lei' sure
length' en
le' ver
lie' o rice
lin ge rie'
lit' er a ture
lon gev' i ty
lu' di crous
lux' u ry
ma lev' o lent
mal treat'
ma ni' a cal
mar' ma lade
mas' sa ere
mat i nee'
me dic' i nal
me di e' val
me' di o ere
mel' an chol y
me men' to
me' ni al
men' u
mer' can tile
mer i to' ri ous
me tic' u lous
min' i a ture
mi rac' u lous
mis' chie vous
mol' e cule
mon' e tary
mo rale'
mo ral' i ty
mu nic' i pal
mu se' um
naph' tha
nar ra' tor
nau' seous
nem' e sis

ni' ce ty
noc tur' nal
no' ta ble
nov' ice
nup' tial
ob lig' a to ry
ob lique'
of' ten
o' gre
om' e let
op pres' sion
or de' al
or' gy
o rig' i nal
pa cif' ic
pac' i fist
par' lia ment
pat' ent
pa' tron age
per' il ous
per' son al
per son nel'
per spi ra' tion
pi an' o
pic' ture
pit' i a ble
pleb' i scite
poign' ant
pol' i tic
pos' i tive ly
pre ced' ence
pre ced' ent (a.)
prec' e dent (n.)
pref' er a bly
pre fer' ment
prel' ate pref ty
prim' i tive
prob' a bly
prod' uce (n.)
pro duce' (v.)
prog' res (n.)
pro gress' (v.)
pro sa' ic

whim' si cal
wit' ti cism

pun' gent
qui' nine
quix ot' ic
rad' ish
ra' tion
re cu' per ate
ref er ee'
ref u gee'
re fuse' (v.)
ref' use (n.)
rep' li ca
rep' u ta ble
re' qui em
re search'
re source'
res' tau rant
ri die' u lous
ro bust'
ro mance'
route
rou tine'
ru' in ous
ruth' less
sat' ire
sched' ule
scru' pu lous
sec re tar' i al
se ere' tive
sen' a tor
ser e nade'
sham poo'
sil hou ette'
sim' i lar
sin' is ter
so' cia ble
sol' dier
squal' id
sta' di urn
sta tis' tics
sta' tus
stra te' gic
strength

xy' lo phone
yeo' ma

stren' u ous
stu pid' i ty
su perb'
su per' flu ous
su preme'
syl' la ble
sym' me try
syn' the sis

tab' er nac le
tac' i turn
tan' gi ble
tern' po rar y
ter rif' ic
tes'ta ment
the' a ter
the ol' o gy
ther mom' e ter
tor' tu ous
trag' e dy
trans par' ent
trav' erse
tre men' dous
tu mul' tu ous
tyr' an ny

ul ti ma' turn
u nan' i mous
u nique'
ur' gen cy
u' ti lize
vac' il lating
val' et
va lise'
vi car' i ous
var ri' e ty
vase
ve' he ment
ve hic' u lar
ver ba' tim
vi' a duct
vi car' i ous
vo' cab u lar y
vul' ner a ble

ze' nith
zeph' yr
zo ol' o gy